ON THE EDGE

THE ART OF HIGH-IMPACT LEADERSHIP

Alison Levine

BUSINESS PLUS

NEW YORK   BOSTON

Business Plus
Hachette Book Group
237 Park Avenue
New York, NY 10017

www.HachetteBookGroup.com

Printed in the United States of America

RRD-C

First Edition: January 2014
10 9 8 7 6 5 4 3 2 1

Business Plus is an imprint of Grand Central Publishing.
The Business Plus name and logo are trademarks of Hachette Book Group, Inc.

The publisher is not responsible for websites (or their content) that are not owned by the publisher.

Library of Congress Cataloging-in-Publication Data
Levine, Alison.
   On the edge : the art of high-impact leadership / Alison Levine.—First edition.
      pages cm
   Includes index.
   ISBN 978-1-4555-4487-5 (hardcover)—ISBN 978-1-4789-2522-4 (audio book)—ISBN 978-1-4789-2523-1 (audio download)—ISBN 978-1-4555-4485-1 (ebook) 1. Levine, Alison. 2. Leadership. 3. Mountaineering.
4. Organizational behavior. 5. Women executives—United States. I. Title.
   HD57.7.L4737 2014
   658.4'092—dc23
                                                    2013026512

*I would like to dedicate this book to the most amazing,
intelligent, handsome, charming, exceptional, loving,
wonderful, talented, brilliant, compassionate, entertaining,
inspiring, incredible living being on the planet—Trooper.
You are the best companion a gal could ever want.
And to Pat, my soul mate, who is all of that and more.
I love you.*

*Also . . . to the beautiful Meg Berté Owen. See you on the
other side, sister. Save me a seat right next to you.*

ACKNOWLEDGMENTS

I would like to thank Jamie Raab, president of Grand Central Publishing, and the team at Business Plus for making this book happen. To Rick Wolff, my publisher and editor—your guidance has been invaluable. Thank you for championing me and for giving me just enough honest advice to make me want to work hard to be a better author, but not so much that I needed therapy. You believed from the beginning that I could write this book myself, and I am glad I listened to you. A few more shout-outs to others at Grand Central to whom I am indebted—Meredith Haggerty, Amanda Pritzker, Bob Castillo, Kristin Vorce, Tracy Brickman, Mark Long, and Karen Andrews—thanks for the editorial help, the publicity efforts, the production work, and the legal perspective.

I also want to thank the dream team at Dupree Miller & Associates (DMA). Jan Miller—literary agent extraordinaire— thank you for agreeing to represent me and for not firing the receptionist who put my call through to you. Nena Madonia—I am not sure where I would be without you (well, chances are I'd still be enjoying life in a tent some- where, but my name wouldn't be on the cover of a book). You held my hand, gave me your ear, and had my back throughout this entire process from start to finish. To the rest of the DMA crew: Shannon Marven, Nicki Miser, Ivonne Ortega, and Lacy Lynch—your efforts are much appreciated.

Maria Shriver, Renee Croce, and Roberta Hollander—thanks to all of you lovely ladies for believing in this book and for connecting me with DMA. And thanks for being lovely.

I could not have pulled together my initial book proposal without the help of Joanne Gordon. Jake Norton, Don Healy, and Garrett Madison were kind enough to supply me with dozens of photos. Clint Willis—I am incredibly grateful for your willingness to help me work through my first draft. The wisdom you shared made this a better book and made me a better writer. Your ability to read my work and make meaningful suggestions for improvement while on your surfboard was nothing short of remarkable. I think there's still a piece of seaweed stuck to page 74.

I'd like to acknowledge Col. Bernie Banks and the entire Department of Behavioral Sciences and Leadership (BS&L) at the United States Military Academy at West Point—thank you for the opportunity to be part of your part-time faculty. It's such an honor to have shared the classroom with you. Col. Diane Ryan—you are a great inspiration and role model to so many cadets, and to me as well. As soon as scientists get the human cloning thing down I'll need to borrow you for a bit, so please start filling out your paperwork to take some leave. Col. (Ret.) Eric Kale—you made the study of leadership both interesting and fun. We miss you in BS&L, but we know you are there in spirit.

To Gen. (Ret.) Tom Kolditz, who is now teaching at Yale but who I first worked with at West Point when he was head of BS&L: You've been an incredible mentor over the years, and I value your advice and friendship more than I could ever express. You are the best resource I know when it comes to leading teams in extreme environments. I feel incredibly lucky that our paths crossed so many years ago and I envy the students at Yale who are benefiting from your knowledge and your passion about the study of leadership.

Dr. Karen Kuhla, Rick Minicozzi, and the rest of the Thayer Leader Development Group at West Point—thank you for the opportunity to work alongside and learn from some of the best leaders in the public and private sectors.

To everyone at the Center on Leadership and Ethics at Duke University—it's an honor to serve on your board and to help develop leaders of consequence. Some of the themes in this book came directly from our discussions and brainstorming sessions.

I also want to give a nod to those who have taught me much about the mountains and polar environments—and there are too many of you to mention, but if I have climbed with you or skied to a pole with you—gracias. Chhewang Nima Sherpa (aka "Trouble")—thank you for being my guardian angel. I know I will see you again.

Janet Hanson—the support from you and the 85 Broads network made climbing many mountains a lot easier. Standing on the shoulders of others always put me closer to the summit.

Thanks to my family—the Levines, Kerns, and Schlenkers.

I'd also like to apologize, in advance, to trees. If it happens that this book sells lots of hard copies—I'm sorry. Thank you for the paper.

And to any company that makes pain relievers—*you're welcome* for the boost in sales brought on by all of the people mentioned above who bought an excess amount of headache remedies throughout the process of helping me make this book a reality.

Alison Levine
Summer 2013

CONTENTS

FOREWORD

Alison Levine knows what adversity looks like. More than that, she knows what it feels like and how it can hurt.

A climber faces some of the most difficult and extreme physical adversities of any athlete—competing with high altitudes, sore muscles, unrelenting fatigue, and unpredictable weather.

So, when I hear Alison say that a person cannot control the environment but only his or her reaction to it, I know I am hearing leadership advice from someone who has been there, someone who has faced some of the most extreme environmental circumstances imaginable.

Many of the leadership lessons Alison articulates in this book are lessons that resonate with me in the work I do with my basketball teams at Duke and with USA Basketball.

I love the way she talks about past experiences—that, whether they be failures or successes, they are essentially irrelevant in the moment. She would say that "It doesn't matter what you've done on a past expedition; all that matters is how you are performing on the mountain now." In my work as a basketball coach, I call that concept "Next Play." Previous plays, games, or seasons must not carry into the current moment. Certainly past mistakes and successes can inform the way a person decides to practice and prepare and get better, but, in the moment, when you are on the mountain, the last expedition just doesn't carry any meaning anymore.

I also really appreciate the way she discusses leadership in sports as compared with leadership in today's business world. In both, there are crucial moments when on-the-spot decisions must be made in reaction to the circumstances you face. I agree with Alison that this is perhaps one of the most important lessons that business leaders can learn from sports leaders, and vice versa.

The way you react to something in the moment will depend heavily on the way in which you prepare to face challenges. Alison will tell you to practice things like sleep deprivation, something my family will tell you is common for me during the basketball season, and certainly, in Alison's adventures, it is a crucial obstacle to overcome. Perhaps sleep deprivation is not a common challenge in your sport, business, or lifestyle, but Alison's point about practice and preparation is vital to anyone's success.

Practice, though, can only be a simulation. You will never be able to replicate exactly what it feels like to be cold and exhausted and still two hundred feet from the peak of a mountain or to have the basketball in your hands down by one point with seconds on the clock. But you can sure try. And one who wants to be ultimately prepared to make it to the top or to sink a game-winning shot will need to do whatever he or she can to make practice feel as real as possible.

Alison and I also share a fondness for teammates with egos, and I love the way she describes the *performance egos* and the *team ego* of her American Women's Everest Expedition team. *Ego* has become a negative word; many see it as being synonymous with arrogance.

To Alison and me, ego is a good thing, and I always want

to surround myself and populate my teams with individuals who have strong, healthy egos. Then, I want all of those people, myself included, to buy into what we are doing together in order to form a collective ego that is greater than any individual ego could ever be. Who we are as a team trumps who any of us are as individuals.

A mountain climb is the consummate metaphor for enduring and, ultimately, achieving. Fighting an "uphill battle" doesn't get any more literal than that. Alison has climbed the highest peaks on every continent. She has endured issues with her health that brought about challenges to her future as an athlete. She has accomplished feats of physical and mental strength that only a handful of human beings have ever even attempted.

So, when she talks about facing challenges and breaking through the barriers of one's perceived limitations, I tend to listen.

I would be lying if I didn't admit that it makes me feel proud that Alison has taken Duke banners to the top of many of the world's highest peaks. But, frankly, more than that, I am proud to know her, to have talked about leadership and teamwork with her, and to have had the honor of contributing to this terrific book about leadership from one of the toughest leaders I know.

—*Mike Krzyzewski, 2013*
Head Coach—Duke University Men's Basketball
and U.S. National Olympic Team

APPROACH

May 17, 2010. Encouraging news. According to the weather forecasters, there will be a good weather window with no jet stream from May 22 to May 26. We want to beat the crowds up high, so we leave Everest base camp at 4:00 a.m. so that we are in position at the South Col to go for the summit when the window opens. We go through the Khumbu Icefall for the second-to-last time. *I will not miss this thing.* I hear a noise coming from above and look toward the sky. I see helicopters flying overhead…and I can make out human figures dangling from haul lines. *Are the figures at the ends of the ropes moving or not?* I can't help but wonder if these are rescues or body recoveries. One of each, I am told. *Either way, that is not a helicopter ride I want to take.* It takes us twelve hours to get to Camp 2. We are not speedy, but we are solid.

I fall into my tent at Camp 2. I am tired. I miss my friends Squash, Wosh, and Ritta—the ones with the funny nicknames whom I have shared a tent with on previous expeditions. Cramming four of us in a tent is, of course, a bit crowded, but Ritta and I are small, so we always make it work. They are my favorite climbing partners, as we always laugh our heads off when we are together. *I wish I were in the mood to laugh right now.* I wish I had someone to encourage me, as I am feeling unsure about whether I can actually make it to the summit. *Meg, where are you? Oh, here you are. I need you to hold my hand. I am sorry I wasn't there to hold yours before you left. I am holding it now....*

We are scheduled to spend two nights at Camp 2 before moving up, in order to recover from the long climb from base camp. Decisions on when to move up are based not only on weather, but also on what other teams are doing. We want to avoid the crowds; waiting on the fixed lines for too long can be dangerous and can jeopardize a summit bid. *What is up with this weather??? Blasting snow, high winds...* We end up staying at Camp 2 longer than expected.

May 21. We leave at 3:30 a.m. for Camp 3. The Lhotse Face is steep and icy, and we are clipped in to the fixed lines for safety the entire time. I remember Peter Legate, who slipped on the Face and died when I was on my previous expedition in 2002. He was a Brit who worked for the BBC. *I will not slip and die, as I am not British. This is good logic.* Peter's climbing partners ran to our camp for help after the accident—we were still down at Camp 2 getting ready to head up. But there was nothing anyone could do. His body succumbed to the trauma of the fall. He sleeps in a crevasse somewhere below the Lhotse Face. It takes me more than nine hours to climb that Face. I am slower than usual. *What is wrong with me?* Must be the extra weight I am carrying—none of which is physical. I arrive at Camp 3 and find Garrett standing outside his tent. He tells me I did a great job getting there. *Liar. I did not perform well today. But I appreciate his encouragement.* Always a smile and a pat on the back. *It helps.* We spend a night at Camp 3, and I have a much better night there than I did during the last rotation. *Thanks to sucking oxygen all night.* We sleep on oxygen and will continue to use it until we get back down from the summit. This is the norm for 98 percent of climbers on Everest. The scary thing is that once you start burning through your Os, the clock is ticking and your timing is no longer flexible. You have essentially started your summit bid because you have a limited amount of oxygen. *I hear the ticking sound. It won't stop.* The tank I am using is much lighter this time—less than half the weight of the tank I used in 2002. This is a really good thing. Carrying less weight means I can move faster. At this elevation, saving weight really matters, and a few extra pounds can make or break you.

May 22. We make our way through the Yellow Band and across the Geneva Spur, and we land at Camp 4 at the South Col in about 6.5 hours. Today was a good day for me. I was much stronger and climbed at a faster clip than I did on my way to Camp 3. For the first time we can really get a good look at the summit pyramid. *How the hell am I going to make it all the way up there???* Now we are above 26,000 feet—in a place called the death zone. The significance of the name is not lost on me. At 26,000 feet human life can no longer be sustained, so our bodies are slowly starting to die. *Yikes.* We tuck ourselves into our tents and suck on oxygen and drift off to sleep. Or perhaps it is just a state of semiconsciousness. Not sure. Doesn't matter really. It feels peaceful.

May 23. Rest day for us, but many teams are moving up already. *Anxious.* We hear reports of long lines of people waiting at the Hillary Step. Apparently the delays are more than ninety minutes. People can get frostbite waiting around like that. I need to eat and hydrate all day so that I have the energy for the big push tomorrow, but it is hard to get food/liquids down once you are in the death zone, because your body is slowly starting to shut down and you have no appetite whatsoever. Best to eat foods that you really like and that are easy to digest. The Sherpas serve us some kind of spicy lentils over rice. *Are they kidding with this food at Camp 4? Who can eat this stuff??? Not me.* I can't get it down. But I remember the story Michael Horst shared with us about the guy who didn't eat the day before his summit attempt and threw his food out the back vestibule of the tent. He didn't have enough energy to climb during the final push, and he didn't make it to the summit. I knew I should not toss my food out the back vestibule of the tent. *I'll toss it out the front.*

Weather reports are still good for tomorrow, so we plan to head out at 11:00 p.m. this evening. Midmorning, a radio call comes in to our Sirdar (the head Sherpa on an expedition), Lakpa Rita. A climber from the Altitude Junkies team is in trouble at the South Summit. Lakpa prepares to go help with the rescue. He grabs an extra tank of oxygen and some syringes of dexamethasone, which may save this climber's life if he has cerebral edema from the extreme altitude. Before I can tell him to stay safe, he is gone—heading up the frozen slopes to assist a climber who is struggling to survive. Lakpa is one of the strongest climbers on the mountain. Everyone knows he has what it takes to save lives up high. He is a hero. He makes it back to the South Col in the late afternoon. I breathe a sigh of relief that he has come back safely. There is a reason he is our head Sherpa. He is superhuman.

We take it easy the rest of the afternoon, mentally preparing for what lies ahead. The hours pass, and the winds start picking up. And up. And up. Our tents are getting battered around a bit. *Can't really be that bad out there. Probably sounds worse than it is from the inside of the tent.* But we should be okay, because we are right smack in the middle of the forecast "window of good weather." So these winds are temporary, I'm sure. *And at least it isn't snowing.*

10:00 p.m. An updated weather report comes in—increased high winds and up to a foot of snow are expected. *WHAT THE???? Our weather guy sucks!!! Okay...I need to relax.... We probably won't go this evening.* There is no way we will climb in this weather. Most of the other teams who were ready to go for it are calling off their summit bids.

10:30 p.m. I hear a voice outside my tent. Chhewang Nima Sherpa is asking if I am ready to go. *You are kidding, right???* Winds are howling and it is snowing and visibility is sh*t. But we are already burning up our oxygen supply, so we need to make a move, and we have already been up in the death zone for more than twenty-four hours, which means our bodies and our brain cells are deteriorating. The Sherpas call for us again. We are going for the summit. I lucked out, because I get to climb alongside Chhewang, who is going for his nineteenth summit—one less than the record held by Apa Sherpa. I am honored to be climbing with such a famous and accomplished guy. He puts his hand on my shoulder, and over the howling wind he asks me if I am ready to climb. *Seriously? In these conditions??? No, I am not ready!* I look him in the eye and tell him, "Yes."

We are all set to leave camp at the Col. Everyone around me looks like an expressionless zombie. But there is plenty of emotion, just not on our frozen faces. Anticipation, hope, excitement, enthusiasm, fear, anxiety. I am acutely aware of all the climbers who have made the tough decision to stay put in the safety of their tents and not attempt to go any higher. Most of them will head back down to base camp in the morning, disappointed that they did not get to take a shot at the top because of the weather. They will feel robbed that their season on Everest will end without a summit. I know that feeling all too well. This mountain and I have a history.

Now the wind is really screaming. Or maybe it's my brain that is screaming, not sure. Most likely it is both. The temperature continues to drop. Even when I'm standing still my face stings from the wind and the ice. But I know I need to start climbing. *How could this possibly get any worse?* At least I know our base camp staff is standing by on radio in case of an emergency.

11:00 p.m. We have lost radio contact with base camp....

——————

My first attempt on Mount Everest was in 2002 when I served as the team captain of the first American Women's Everest Expedition, which was sponsored by the Ford Motor Company. Our team came within a couple hundred feet of the top of the mountain when we were forced to turn back because of deteriorating weather conditions. Although we didn't get to the summit, it was a phenomenal experience—but one that I swore I would never repeat. Once was enough. I didn't really feel the need to spend another two months on that mountain (not to mention all the time I would need to put into training prior to the climb) just to take in the views from the very tippy-top; the views from the South Summit at 28,700 feet above sea level were spectacular enough. Going a few hundred feet farther wasn't going to change my world or anybody else's. I honestly felt like I had the whole "Everest experience" already. Yet there I was, eight years later, back on that mountain, *in the same exact situation*, ready to go for the top—and in comes a storm *again*.

But we can't control the environment; all we can control is the way we react to it. Most people positioned at the high camp the night of May 23, 2010, abandoned their summit attempt, as my team did back in 2002 when the jet stream got the best of us. And while I found myself in a similarly harrowing position during round two on Everest, the entire experience was remarkably different. This time, I was a better climber. Not because I was physically stronger at age forty-four than I was at age thirty-six, because I wasn't. But the second time around I had the advantage of another eight years of mountaineering experience under my belt (or rather, my climbing harness). I had also done some extreme ski expeditions across Antarctica and the Arctic Circle, which further helped me gauge my risk tolerance and my pain threshold. But more than anything, what really helped me handle myself well on the mountain was the knowledge I had gained about *leadership*. This book is about those lessons.

There is no shortage of leadership books written by presidents, politicians, CEOs, psychologists, military heroes, and executive coaches. I am none of the above. My take on leadership comes primarily from my experiences as a high-altitude mountaineer and polar explorer. In addition to serving as the team captain of the first American Women's Everest Expedition, I have climbed the highest peak on every continent (the Seven Summits) and skied to both the North and South Poles, an achievement known as the

Adventure Grand Slam.* My adventures have taken me to some of the harshest, most remote places on the planet, where determination is every bit as important as skill when it comes to survival.

Almost all of my expeditions have been fraught with hurdles brought about by harsh conditions, malfunctioning equipment, difficult climbing partners, and logistical mishaps—not to mention my own health issues. I was born with a life-threatening heart condition that has required three surgical procedures. I also suffer from a circulatory disease that affects my blood vessels and puts me at high risk of frostbite—so doctors have always told me to avoid cold environments. I guess I don't always listen. The stories in this book document how I approached and tackled these various challenges and illustrate many of the principles I followed. Or wish I had followed.

Off the mountain, as a leadership development consultant and keynote speaker, I have addressed hundreds of global organizations in the midst of their own marketplace and workplace challenges. This book's insights also reflect my two decades working with and speaking to leaders in

---

* There is some controversy as to what qualifies as completing the Adventure Grand Slam when it comes to reaching the North and South Poles. Many adventurers claim to have completed it by starting out at 89 degrees and skiing the last degree (approximately sixty-nine miles) to each of the Poles. A "last degree" trip usually takes ten to fourteen days. Others claim that in order to complete the Grand Slam a "full crossing" is required, which means starting from an accepted coastal point and skiing several hundred miles over a period of approximately six to eight weeks to reach the Pole. Fewer than forty people have completed the Adventure Grand Slam. Roughly twenty-four skiers have done so by last degree, and ten have done so by a full crossing. I skied the last degree to the North Pole and did a full crossing to the South Pole.

business, politics, sports, and academia, as well as my work as an adjunct professor at the United States Military Academy at West Point in the Department of Behavioral Sciences and Leadership. There, I had the privilege of working side by side with top academic and military faculty to help the West Point cadets prepare for the life-and-death situations they may face while serving our country as army officers once they graduate.

On the Edge is a handbook for *everyone*: senior executives, junior executives, politicians, administrative personnel, educators, and students. It is for mothers and fathers and athletes and coaches. Good, sound leadership is necessary not just in corporate environments and government buildings but at home, in schools, and on playing fields.

Everyone is in a leadership position—regardless of age or title or tenure or where we work. Leadership has nothing to do with salary level or how many people report to you or how much revenue you produce or how large of a budget you oversee. I don't care whether you've worked for a particular firm for ten years or ten months or ten minutes.

Leadership is everyone's responsibility. It is not solely the responsibility of the C-level executives or the management team within an organization. We are all in a position to proactively work toward having a positive effect on the people around us. Everyone in an organization is responsible for helping to move forward with the mission; but in addition, all employees/teammates/people must realize it is also their responsibility to look out for the people on either side of them and to help those people move in the right direction as well.

Granted, the challenges that most folks come up against in their companies, careers, and everyday lives rarely present the same physical dangers that mountaineers or polar explorers encounter. But while the surroundings are completely different, many of the lessons learned have strong applicability in both settings. Few could argue that we are indeed living in extreme times. Our economic, governmental, social, technological, and environmental landscapes are constantly shifting and changing. Every organization's budgets are tight, resources are slim, and markets move at a breakneck pace. The result is unprecedented volatility and risk for companies as well as their employees. More than ever, there is intense pressure to not just survive but to thrive. And just as it's easy to get lost on a mountain during a sudden whiteout and lose sight of the summit, it's also easy to get lost in the unpredictable chaos of modern-day life and lose sight of our personal and professional aspirations as well as our responsibilities to those around us.

Of course when you are high up in the death zone on a big Himalayan peak or are crossing hundreds of miles of polar ice on skis, underperforming isn't about losing market share. It's about losing lives, or perhaps a few critical body parts. The stakes are high when there is *real* flesh in the game, and therefore the leaders I find most intriguing are not necessarily the people at the helm of America's most admired companies; they are the people who enable teams to survive and thrive in extreme environments. And I've been lucky enough to have had the opportunity to learn from some of the best.

Leadership in extreme environments requires the willpower, the teamwork, the high moral character, and the emotional intelligence necessary to overcome exceptional hurdles, solve complex problems, and face any sudden, uncontrollable, high-risk situation, including those that exist in today's business world. The global economy is more unpredictable than ever, and we each have more on the line as we try to navigate its shifting terrain: careers, reputations, financial futures, perhaps even lives. The potential costs of a mistake—be they professional, monetary, or emotional—can be high if we do not make the right choices.

The leadership principles that apply in extreme adventure sports also apply in today's extreme business environments. Both settings require you to be able to make crucial decisions on the spot when the conditions around you are far from perfect. Your survival—and the survival of your team—depends on it.

My hope is that this book will serve as an engaging leadership manual through concrete insights and lessons—applicable to business as well as to other aspects of life. I intend to provide a framework to help people scale whatever big peaks—literal or figurative—they aspire to climb by sharing my practical, humorous (sometimes…sort of…), and often unorthodox advice about how to grow as a leader. I'm opening my entire playbook for you—something I can't do from the podium during a formal keynote presentation. I'm giving you all the bits and pieces that I tend to hold back when I'm addressing the senior management of a Big 4 accounting firm during its annual partners meeting, where I really have to watch my p's and q's. You will find my approach candid, direct, and perhaps even politically incorrect, because that's how people tend to talk to each other when there's no one from human resources around. And be forewarned…some of my advice is flat-out contrarian. It may fly in the face of other books or advice from your highly paid executive coach.

Here are just a few pieces of advice that may seem a little baffling at first glance:

- Look for teammates with big egos.
- When you're making progress, turn around and change direction.
- Practice sleep deprivation.
- Don't try to overcome weakness.
- Success can be a problem.

But I promise you that there is method to my madness and a rationale behind these recommendations. The information compiled in this book isn't just from my own expedition arsenal; I have assembled advice and stories from some phenomenal leaders who show why these practices make sense. Most of these people have never read Jack Welch's books, nor do they subscribe to the *Harvard Business Review*, but they know how to lead when lives are on the line.

Developing yourself as a leader should be a deliberate, conscious process. Think about how much time and energy (and dollars) people spend on achieving optimal physical health—yet few people put the time and effort into strengthening their leadership skills. Just as building muscle strength requires a repetitive routine, the more time you spend focusing on your leadership skills, the stronger they will become. Think P90X, but for leadership instead of your abs.

This book will help you build your "leadership muscles." That doesn't happen as a result of getting a new title or a promotion, or by working a set number of years for an organization. None of these things have anything to do with leadership.

Leadership is an attitude. Every one of us on this planet is in a leadership position. We all have a responsibility to help one another. If you look at what's happening in the world today, I think you'll agree that the challenges are huge, but the opportunities are even greater. What we say matters. What we do makes a difference. *And how we lead has impact.* We all need to be better leaders. If we put some effort into that, there is no limit to the amount of positive influence we can have on the people around us.

Alison Levine
2013

Disclaimer: I have described the various events that took place on my expeditions over the years to the best of my recollection. Some of the names and identities have been changed. It is possible that there are minor errors in this book, which I assure you are unintentional. Some of the entries from my expedition blogs were slightly tweaked in order to correct grammar and spelling (it's not always easy to get that stuff right at altitude). If there are any glaring errors or omissions, they are probably the fault of my ghost-writer. Her name is Alison Levine, in case you would like to direct any complaints her way.

Chapter 1

HARD-CORE PREPARATION

Sometimes It Hurts

I believe in being prepared. But when I say, "be prepared," I don't necessarily mean what other people mean when they utter the Boy Scout motto. I'm not talking about bringing extra matches. I'm talking about *extreme* preparation.

On May 16, 1975, Junko Tabei reached the summit of Mount Everest and became the first woman to stand on top of the world's highest mountain. She was four foot nine, thirty-five years old, and had a two-year-old daughter at home in Tokyo at the time. What made her accomplishment even more remarkable was that twelve days earlier, she and four of her teammates—all part of a Japanese women's expedition—had been caught in an avalanche at Camp 2 and were completely buried. It took six Sherpas to dig them out. Miraculously, they all survived, but their bodies were beaten up and bruised, as were their psyches. Junko herself was in so much pain immediately after the avalanche that she could barely stand. Still, something got her to the summit. *What was it?* Here's what Tabei will tell you: "Technique and ability alone do not get you to the top—it is the willpower that is the most important. This willpower you cannot buy with money or be given by others—it rises from your heart."

Fair enough, but I would add this: while willpower may help you get you to the top, you better have technique and ability if you plan to get yourself and your team back down. People often forget that the top is only the halfway point. The majority of deaths on big peaks occur *after* people have reached the summit, because they have used every ounce of energy they have to get to the top and have nothing left to get themselves back down. The descent on Everest's summit ridge is harrowing—it's a 10,000-foot drop on one side and an 8,000-foot drop on the other. You have to descend the infamous Hillary Step, a forty-foot spur of near-vertical rock and ice at 28,740 feet, and make it back down to the South Col at 26,300 feet, so you better have enough reserves—both in your oxygen tank and in your body. Otherwise? You'll die.

The cruel fact is that many people who are absolutely, categorically determined to succeed on Everest die on the mountain because they're not ready for the reality they encounter on the peak. In fact, sheer desire accompanied by a lack of preparation is often a deadly concoction up there. Tabei was right on the money when she said that you need mental toughness to get to the top, but rarely is it enough by itself: in extreme environments you will vastly increase your odds of success if you add proper training and preparation.

Over the years I have seen many expeditions end in disappointment because of a lack of preparedness. If you're going to take on a big, hairy challenge, be it in the mountains, in business, or in life, you understand up front that you may succeed or you may not. But you don't ever want to fail and wonder if the outcome would have been different had you only been more ready. When you get shut down because of environmental factors, you face disappointment, but you don't second-guess yourself or your abilities, since the environment is something that you cannot do anything about. But if you turn back short of your goal because you just weren't strong enough to make it, that's when you start to beat yourself up and ask the tough questions: *Could I have trained more? Trained harder? Trained smarter? Was I dedicated enough? Was I focused enough?*

Only you can answer these questions. You want to go into a climb feeling as if you have done everything humanly possible to set yourself and your team up for success, because once you get to the mountain everything is working against you: the cold, the wind, the altitude, the physical deterioration, the psychological challenges, the teammate who steals your extra toilet paper—everything. There is no excuse for showing up in less than top form. You owe it to yourself, and more important, you owe it to your team. Leaders have got to show up ready for battle. People will expect more from you than they do from others. You need to be able to perform at a level, both physically *and* psychologically, that exceeds expectations.

High-altitude expedition training is no easy task for anyone, but it is especially challenging for those who don't live near the mountains and have to find alternative ways to get into shape—people like me. In 2001, when I was preparing for the first American Women's Everest Expedition, I was just one year out of business school and was a new associate at Goldman Sachs. I had just transferred to the firm's

San Francisco office after spending nine months at its head-quarters in New York City. Getting a job at Goldman came as a shock to me. I had competed with applicants who had Ivy League educations, and many of them had worked in finance prior to earning their MBAs. I was liberal arts major at the University of Arizona and had no finance or account-ing background. The fact that I didn't do particularly well in my quantitative classes in business school made getting a job at a blue-chip financial firm seem even less likely. But I did have tenacity, drive, and determination. I also sent post-cards to the firm's recruiters every time I went on a climb-ing trip during my vacation time from business school, so I think I scored some creativity points there (as that stands out more than sending a postcard from a CFA* class). And the people who made the hiring decisions had faith that I was at least intelligent enough to learn the business.

I had gone to business school with the intent of opening an adventure travel company someday, and working for an investment bank was not what I had envisioned for myself. But I did want to learn about finance, and to that end, I figured there was no better place than a Wall Street firm. Not surprisingly, I was out of my comfort zone every day in that job at Goldman. I was surrounded by people who truly had a passion for the markets. Most of my colleagues were at their desks by 5:00 or 6:00 a.m., and many came in even earlier. I wasn't really all that sure what they were doing there that early every day, but everyone looked busy, which wasn't hard to do—you could just stare at your computer

---

* The CFA—Chartered Financial Analyst designation—is a credential that represents in-depth knowledge of the investment industry. Candi-dates must complete the required coursework and pass three six-hour exams. It takes an average of four years to complete the program.

screen and either nod or shake your head excessively based on what the markets were doing.

I really wanted to do well at the firm; after all, landing the job in the first place was such a long shot, and I didn't want to disappoint the people who had gone out on a limb to hire me. I was sure that they would eventually figure out they had made the hiring mistake of the century, but I didn't want to blow it right away, so I came in early and worked late and pretended that I had what it took to get meetings with important people. I would pick up the phone and speak at an abnormally loud volume level for the benefit of the people who were seated around me in the office. "Yes, yes, Mr. Gates…well, okay, *Bill*…if you insist…yep, looking forward to seeing you on Tuesday. Yep, ten a.m. works great. Give my best to Melinda."

Of course there was no one on the other end of the phone. I couldn't seem to get any business prospects to meet with me. That might have been why I never earned a penny of commission and made less money than most of the administrative assistants there. Then again, they were better at their jobs than I was at mine. But while I felt incredibly out of place at Goldman, I was also determined to make it work. I was learning a lot, and although I truly sucked at the job, I really liked the firm and the people. And whether I enjoyed the work was irrelevant—I had signed up for the job, and I didn't want to fail.

Things got even trickier when the markets took a nosedive in 2001. Everyone was worried about layoffs, so work turned into a huge face-time contest. Everyone started coming in earlier and earlier and staying later and later. No one wanted to be the last one in or the first to leave. I was now getting home around 8:00 p.m.

Meanwhile, I was still trying to find a corporate sponsor for the Everest expedition, because there would be no trip unless I raised the funds. I didn't have $30,000 lying around, and no one else I knew who was a climber had any money, either. In addition, I was also trying to raise money for the V Foundation for Cancer Research, an organization founded by ESPN and legendary college basketball coach Jim Valvano, who died of cancer in 1993. I was a big fan of Valvano because of his "Never Give Up" speech, which he delivered during ESPN's ESPY (Excellence in Sports Performance Yearly) Awards just eight weeks before he died. I wanted this climb to have some impact and figured that was a good way to do it.

Of course, I was banking on the fact that the Everest expedition was actually going to happen, so there was some pressure to ensure the trip became a reality, since I had already told the V Foundation I was climbing in honor of Coach Valvano. So I would get home from work, open my mail, get some food in me, and then I'd spend what was left of the evening focused on finding an expedition sponsor and on soliciting donations for cancer research. I was writing dozens of letters and sending out hundreds of e-mails each night. By the time I thought about looking up at the clock it was already midnight—often later. I had to get up at 4:00 a.m. every morning, which left me about four hours each night to both sleep *and* train to climb the world's highest peak.

I eventually came up with what I thought was an ideal solution to this conundrum. I found a health club that was open twenty-four hours, and I would go there around 1:00 in the morning and find cardio equipment that I could do with my eyes closed (StairMaster with a heavy pack, or stationary bike with a lot of resistance). As I was stepping or pedaling away, I tried to convince myself that during my visits to the gym I was both sleeping *and* working out *at the same time*. I figured that if I could build some leg strength, work on my cardio, and also get some REM sleep in before the sun came up, it was a pretty good use of my "free time." I congratulated myself for being a master multitasker. Ha!

Of course I wasn't accomplishing either of the things I needed to be doing (sleeping or training properly), and the exhaustion caught up to me after about ten days. Meanwhile, my stress level was through the ceiling. I was compromising my health by existing in a chronic state of sleep deprivation and extreme exhaustion. And worse, I wasn't training efficiently, which meant I risked showing up for the climb unprepared. Not an option. As the team captain of the first American Women's Everest Expedition, I couldn't afford for that to happen. But I had to stay focused on the job as well, or I would find myself without one. Also not an option. My paycheck barely covered my monthly living expenses, and I was carrying student loan debt, so I couldn't afford to be unemployed. I needed to remain focused at work because I absolutely could *not* lose my job, and I needed to be focused on the training because people would be counting on me during the expedition.

Ultimately, I knew I had to give up the 1:00 a.m. gym workouts, which weren't cutting it anyway. You can't prepare your body (or your mind) for a serious expedition in a gym. I knew my teammates would be training outdoors in Colorado and Washington State, and I owed it *to them*, as well as to myself, to show up in the best possible shape that I could. With that in mind, I completely changed my training regimen. During the weekdays I stayed totally focused on my job at Goldman and tried to get as much sleep at night as I could, given my 5:30 a.m. start time. I focused on fund-raising in the evenings after work. And then I dedicated my weekends to training properly for the climb. I would work a full day in the office on Friday, and then on Saturday I would drive up to Mount Shasta in Siskiyou County, California—a five-and-a-half- or six-hour drive from my apartment in San Francisco.

The summit of Mount Shasta is 14,179 feet above sea level, and the mountain is covered in snow in the winter. The total distance of the trail from the parking lot to the summit is six miles and the elevation gain is more than 7,000 feet (that's a lot of gain in six miles). A good portion of the route is steep enough to require an ice axe and crampons. Winds on the peak can exceed 100 miles per hour. All in all, Shasta is great conditioning for a serious expedition. Climbing it was certainly much better than anything I could do in a gym.

Training for hours on a StairMaster indoors is incredibly helpful if you're planning to, oh, I don't know, climb a lot of stairs in your temperature-controlled office building—but it won't do squat for you if you're planning to climb an 8,000-meter peak.* If you want to do well on a climb, it's important to simulate the conditions you're going to face on the mountain. That means you have to get outside, strap a heavy pack on your back, grab your ice axe, and go fight your way up some big hills in snow, high winds, and cold temperatures.

Mount Shasta was an ideal training ground for me. I would

---

* There are fourteen peaks in the world that are more than 8,000 meters in height, and they are collectively known as the *8,000-meter peaks* or the *eight thousanders*.

drive up there in the early evening, get there by 11:00 p.m., start the climb around 11:30 p.m., and go from the parking lot to the summit and back in one straight shot—which usually took me ten to twelve hours (depending on how much weight I was carrying). The physical training was right on target. But climbing Shasta also gave me something else— the psychological training that comes with pushing yourself through an entire night with no sleep and knowing you can run on fumes, powered by nothing more than adrenaline and maybe a power gel or two.

Climbing through the night with no sleep is something you frequently do on expeditions. Sometimes you don't sleep because you feel sick from the altitude. Sometimes you don't sleep because the winds are howling all night. Sometimes you don't sleep because your tent mate is snoring like hell. But often you don't sleep because you are starting your climb at 2:00 a.m. (perhaps even earlier). Teams start climbing well before sunup; the route is safer when it's frozen, because there is less chance of crevasses opening up or avalanches being triggered or rocks falling with enough momentum to kill you. So even if you lay down in your tent at 9:00 p.m., all you do is toss and turn and stress out about oversleeping.

To be an effective leader, it's important that you condition yourself for the times when sleep is not an option. And there *will* be such times, because that is the nature of changing environments, where the unexpected lies around the corner. When you've got a tight deadline, or you've made a commitment to deliver something, you make good on that commitment even if it means staying up all night to make it happen. It's also highly possible that you may face a crisis situation that calls for round-the-clock attention. It's usually the *stress* of not sleeping that works against people more than the sleep deprivation itself, so that's why it's great to learn you can go a night without getting any z's and still perform the next day. Sure, you perform better with sleep, but if you "practice" sleep deprivation, then you won't stress out when you actually experience it. So you can either be stressed *and* sleep deprived, or just sleep deprived. Take your pick.

You don't ever want to fail because you were too tired. It's just not a good excuse. You have to find that voice inside your head that tells you that you can keep going, and that's when your adrenaline kicks in. Warning: the adrenaline thing may not happen when you're sitting in your office waiting for your 4:00 p.m. meeting to go over the financials from last quarter, so there are times when a cup of coffee might be warranted. I also highly recommend perfecting the art of the power nap. Go out to your car or close the door to your office, and sleep for twenty minutes. Dr. Jonathan Friedman, director of the Texas Brain and Spine Institute, claims that "emerging scientific evidence suggests that naps—even very short ones—significantly enhance cognitive function." There you have it.

I know there will be someone who will read this and tell me that the idea of practicing sleep deprivation contradicts what the American Academy of [*insert your favorite medical specialty here*] states in some white paper or journal article about how to stay healthy and perform well. I get it—I'm not arguing that. I am simply telling you what works for me. Take it or leave it. Yes, I've read many of the scientific studies about sleep deprivation affecting performance and judgment, and I am aware that researchers have found that a prolonged period of sleep deprivation has the same cognitive effects as a 0.10 blood alcohol level,* which is above the legal limit for driving in every state in America.

But you're not operating a motor vehicle on Everest, and this book isn't about how to live to be a hundred. It's about how to do what you need to do when your team is relying on you. As a leader, if you are stressed out about something as minor as being tired, your team will also feel stressed out. I'm not saying it's good for you not to sleep. I am just saying that in extreme situations you will need to function when sleep deprived. So don't let the fact that you haven't slept before a tough day on the trail (or in the office) create unnecessary anxiety. Just push through it. It's a short-term thing. It's temporary.

In addition to conditioning myself for sleep deprivation, Mount Shasta also allowed me to do what I call caloric deprivation training. I practiced climbing while dehydrated and calorie deprived. I purposely did not drink enough or eat enough during the twelve-hour push so that I would know what it felt like to have to climb in that kind of physical condition. Of course I kept plenty of water and food in my backpack in case I truly needed it. But I wanted to practice climbing when I was running on empty so that my body and my mind would know what that felt like, and I wouldn't feel uneasy about it if I were in that situation on Everest.

The reality is that most people will find themselves climbing in a state of dehydration and caloric deprivation many times during an expedition. There will be times when you need water or calories and you can't get them. And it sucks

---

* Williamson, A. M. and Anne-Marie Feyer, "Moderate Sleep Deprivation Produces Impairments in Cognitive and Motor Performance Equivalent to Legally Prescribed Levels of Alcohol Intoxication," *Occupational and Environmental Medicine* 57, no. 10 (October 2000): 649–655.

when you pull a candy bar out of your pocket after keeping it warm for seven hours so that you can bite into it without losing a tooth, only to have it slip out of your gloved hand and sail down the snowy slopes of the mountain. And it's a huge bummer to not be able to drink from your water bottle because it's frozen solid, even though it was in an insulated bottle holder that the guy at the gear store swore would keep it from turning to ice. You need to know what it feels like to have to push yourself through discomfort so that you can keep going during those most intense and demanding climbing days.

Once you've been there—in that place of feeling like you've got nothing left, and you've pressed right on through it—you know you can do it again and you aren't worried about it. Climbing big peaks involves pushing yourself to the point where you feel like you just cannot take one more step....And you might say to yourself, *Ohhhhh maaaaann...I don't think I can do this. There is no way I can keep going....* But then you *do* take one more step...and then one more after that. And one more. You go past the point where you think you can go. Then the next time you get to that same point where you think you cannot go *one more step*, you say to yourself, *Okay, I have been here before—where I felt like I was at my limit, and I kept going. I did it before, so I can do it again.* And you take the step. And then you take more of them. And no matter how uncomfortable it gets, you suck it up and you keep going, because it isn't about you. It's about the people around you. You got that? In the end, you train hard for *them.* You do it for your team.

Training isn't always fun. It can feel monotonous and sometimes it can feel lonely. That's why I also recommend finding good training partners. Not just because having company can make it more fun, but because it'll help improve your skills. It's always preferable to train with people who can withstand the elements and who will push you to do the same. You want to get out on the route with people who are better and stronger than you are; you yourself can become better and stronger by observing others who are more experienced and more skilled. If you spend your time training with people who are slower and less proficient, you aren't going to personally improve. Identify folks who are going to push you and make you push yourself, and spend as much time as you can observing their technique and absorbing information from them. If you're training to be a surgeon, you assist more seasoned surgeons during their procedures in the operating room before you have a go at a live patient yourself. If you're a basketball player, you get out on the court and practice with players who challenge you on every possession before you play in a big game. If you surround yourself with talented people and you're willing to learn from them, your skills will improve and you *will* get better.

Whether you're trying to become a better climber or a stronger leader or both, one of the best things you can do for yourself is find mentors and spend time learning from them. One of my mentors is Vern Tejas, who has completed the Seven Summits ten times and has climbed Mount McKinley fifty-two times (including the first successful winter solo climb of McKinley in 1988). He's a legend on that mountain. So when I decided I wanted to climb Mount McKinley in 2000, who do you think I chose to climb with? Yep—Vern. I knew he could teach me things that others could not. He is one of the best leaders you could ever ask for. He's a great teacher and mentor, and he makes it clear that he doesn't succeed unless you succeed.

Don't wait for mentors to come to you. Seek them out. Pick people whom you respect and admire, and ask them if you can observe what they do and work alongside them. And don't just look for people who are senior to you. Find ambitious people who are *junior to you*, as you will learn a lot from them as well. This is one way you prepare to lead—by studying, by observing, and by engaging the right mentors.

Another person who taught me a tremendous amount about leadership is Michael Horst, whom I met on Everest in 2010. At age thirty-two he was one of the younger guides on the mountain, yet his leadership style was that of a seasoned veteran, which made him someone I wanted to learn from. Michael was guiding a private climb but was on our permit, so he shared our camps and logistics support. In addition to focusing on the climber who had hired him, he was constantly assisting others. He was always offering to help people carry their gear when they were exhausted, lending people his warmer gloves and clothing when they were cold, and showing up with a packet of energy gel when he saw someone bonking. (As in "hitting the wall." I know you Brits use the term to describe something else, and that is *not* what I'm referencing here, so stop smirking.)

One day on my way to Camp 2, I stopped at the lip of a crevasse because it looked too wide for me to jump over. As I stood there silently cursing my short legs, Michael saw my hesitation and came over to me, reached out his hand, and said, "Come on, we'll jump it together." And we did. Michael Horst worked hard to ensure everyone else's success, and that's something we should all emulate. When you see someone who's nervous about making a huge leap— reach out.

We can learn a lot about leadership from studying other people's good habits and success stories. We can also learn a lot from paying attention to other people's missteps. The race to the South Pole is one of the all-time historic journeys that has always intrigued me, because of the leadership lessons that can be learned from it. Norwegian explorer Roald Amundsen led a five-man team to the South Pole on December 14, 1911, marking the first time human beings reached that desolate spot. While these adventurous Norwegians were making their way across the icy continent, a British team led by Robert F. Scott was attempting to beat the Norwegians to the Pole. Scott and his men got there thirty-four days after Amundsen's team, and they found the Norwegian flag already flapping in the wind. By this time the British group was starving, exhausted, and, needless to say, totally heartbroken and shocked to discover that the Norwegians had won the race. But here's the most tragic part of the story: Scott's men perished on the return trip—just eleven miles from a supply depot of food and gear that could have saved their lives. Their bodies were not discovered until the following summer.

Why did they lose the race? And why did they die? For starters, Scott's men hadn't trained adequately on skis prior to the trip and therefore were not strong enough skiers to be efficient on the Antarctic ice. In contrast, Amundsen's men were proficient skiers and could move swiftly. But not only were Scott's men physically unprepared for the challenge, they also suffered setbacks along the journey because they relied mostly on ponies and manpower to haul all of their gear and supplies. The ponies didn't do well on the Antarctic terrain. Their hooves punched through the ice, and they became weak and ill; eventually, all died of exhaustion or had to be destroyed. Scott's team also brought along a few motorized sledges, but those failed in the cold, and the person who really knew most about how they operated was not with them, so no one really understood the equipment or how to fix it when it broke down. They had some dogs with them, but not nearly enough. Amundsen's team had more than twice as many dogs as Scott's team had, and his men were much more experienced dog handlers and mushers, which worked to his advantage. Basically, lack of skill and lack of knowledge led to the demise of Scott's team on their ill-fated journey. In other words, they weren't prepared.

Of course even if you're ultra-prepared, unfortunate events can still occur, and often they happen at the most inopportune times. One of the most important keys to successful performance, whether inside your team's cluster of cubicles or inside the emergency snow shelter you've just built, is empowering everyone on the team to think and act like a leader. That means helping them hone their skills, working with them to increase their knowledge, and encouraging them to think on their own and make critical decisions without always requiring your input. If something does happen to the designated leader, the team must be able to carry on. Like I said at the beginning of this book, leadership is not solely the responsibility of C-level executives or a management team within an organization. It is not just the job of mountain guides, coaches, team owners, or team captains. In extreme environments, each of us must feel responsible for those around us and should constantly consider how our actions—or inaction—affect others.

Designated leaders need to cultivate leadership skills in each team member by giving others the confidence, the tools, the freedom, and the accountability that empowers each person to take on more responsibility and to make critical decisions when the path ahead may not be clear-cut—especially if the designated leader is no longer able to do the job. What happens when a leader is injured or for some reason is unable to continue to lead? Does the whole team just throw up their arms and say, "Okay, now we're really screwed"? Let's hope not.

Millions of Americans are familiar with the 1996 Everest disaster. Someone could write an entire book about what went wrong (oh, wait—thanks, Jon Krakauer!). Among other things, once the team leaders were no longer around during that deadly storm high up on Mount Everest, no one else really knew what to do. They knew how to take direction from a leader, but they didn't know how to lead. They didn't know how to react when the situation didn't follow what was outlined ahead of time in the playbook. People were lost. So were lives.

You need to develop a strong team by allowing others to lead. Empower others to take on responsibility and to make critical decisions regardless of tenure or experience level. This not only helps to develop leadership skills in others, but it also makes your job easier because others are sharing more of the workload.

For example, in 2008 I was part of an international team of polar explorers that reached the South Pole on skis after a six-week ski traverse across west Antarctica (more on that in chapter 6). We had to cover nearly six hundred miles of frozen terrain on skis while hauling all our gear and supplies in sleds that were harnessed to our waists. We couldn't afford any mistakes, as rescues are very difficult to orchestrate in Antarctica—perhaps the harshest environment known to man. Rescues on the ice can take days, weeks, sometimes months—and our team had to be prepared to survive on its own.

One of the factors that led to our success was that our leader, Eric Philips, had everyone on the team take turns leading the group and navigating the icy terrain. We routinely traded off the position in the front of the line and navigated by our shadows, by compass, and by GPS. It was daunting and empowering, and we all became more adept because of the exercise. If something had happened to Eric, I felt comfortable that our team would not have perished on the ice.

Good leaders understand it's their duty to develop leadership skills in others by routinely asking team members to step into roles of greater responsibility so that they grow as leaders themselves. Doing so not only makes the whole team more effective, but it also prepares the team for worst-case scenarios, which in extreme environments are not all that uncommon.

File under "Extreme Preparation"

Proper preparation includes both physical and psychological training. Engage mentors who are more skilled than you are; learn from the best. Empower your team so that they are able to move forward with the mission whether you are there or not. Developing your skills and the skills of others should be a never-ending process.

Chapter 2

GO BACK, JACK, DO IT AGAIN

Why Backward Is Often the Right Direction

A great fallacy regarding progress is that it is defined by constant forward motion in the same direction. We assume that any steps in the opposite direction take us further from our goal. Not true, especially at high altitudes or in other extreme environments, where the problems and inherent challenges are especially complex. Getting to the top of Mount Everest, for example, generally requires a great deal of time climbing *backward*—away from the summit.

If you were to plug the route to the summit in to Map-Quest, you'd see that there are more than a dozen routes you can take. (Seriously, did you really just ask MapQuest for directions to the summit of Mount Everest?) And while the routes may all begin at different points on the mountain, they of course all end up at the same place—29,029 feet/8,848 meters. (Note: The actual height of Mount Everest is in dispute. Some countries recognize it as 29,029 feet while others believe it is 29,035 feet. Either way, it's a big mountain.) But regardless of which route you decide to take up Mount Everest, the climb is never straightforward.

Just getting to base camp has its challenges. Both times I climbed Everest I did so from the south side of the mountain—the Nepal side. The adventure begins in Kathmandu. From there you take a plane to a village called Lukla. Lukla Airport has been called the "most dangerous airport in the world." The runway is a mere 1,600 feet long and 65 feet wide, and is suitable only for helicopters and small fixed-wing planes. There's a 2,000-foot drop at the end of the runway, which further adds to the danger. Worse, the elevation is more than 9,000 feet, which makes the short runway even more sketchy, given that an aircraft's lift and engine power are reduced at higher altitudes because of the lower atmospheric pressure. And then there is the constant inclement weather and heavy fog, which often delay flights in and out of Lukla for days. If you manage to get on a flight to Lukla within forty-eight hours of your scheduled departure, consider yourself lucky. If you land safely in Lukla, consider yourself even luckier.

Once you get there, the real fun begins as you start the trek to Everest base camp. The thirty-eight-mile trek is popular among global travelers, because it is both scenically breathtaking and culturally fascinating. (The Khumbu Valley is home to the Sherpa.) It's a challenging trek and requires some legs and some lung capacity—as well as a lot of hand sanitizer, because some of the teahouses are filthy and the conditions in the latrines can be pretty horrendous. It's not unusual for trekkers or climbers to pick up a gastrointestinal bug that leads to vomiting and what can only be described as explosive diarrhea (sorry, I realize that isn't a great visual). Some people get such a severe case that they have to end the trek early. Often too weak to walk down, they go out on the backs of mules with oxygen masks strapped across their faces (the people, not the mules). Plenty of Everest dreams have been dashed by GI infections. Nonetheless, the Everest base camp trek remains the most popular trek in the region, and thousands of people flock to walk the trails every year.

There are two types of people you run into during the journey to Everest base camp: trekkers and climbers. The trekkers are there to enjoy the Khumbu region, and many go all the way to base camp. Once they get there they spend a few hours tooling around camp, have some tea, and then they head out and start the walk back to Lukla, which generally takes a few days. These folks get wonderful exposure to the Khumbu region, the Sherpas, and the local culture. And they learn what it feels like to struggle to breathe the thin air above 17,000 feet. The other types that you find on the trail are those who are there to climb Everest, Lhotse, Pumori, or one of the other Himalayan giants situated nearby. For these climbers, the hard work really starts once they reach base camp. This group considers the thirty-eight-mile trek in at high altitude just a walk in the park (well, technically it actually *is* a walk in the park—Sagarmatha National Park).

For me, the trek was an opportunity to clear my head and to mentally prepare for the coming task of getting up that big hill. In 2002 I had almost no idea what to expect, since it was my first experience in the region, but eight years later I had a much better sense of what lay ahead. I was watching reruns in my head from my 2002 expedition—analyzing what went right and what went wrong and thinking about what I would do differently this time around.

While I tried to go into the trek with a clear head each time, it was impossible to not think about the challenge ahead and how one small mishap could end the trip before the real climb even began. All the effort put into physical training, finding sponsors and raising the funds to pay for the trip, organizing the logistics, and getting all of the required gear and supplies together (some people spend *years* preparing for an Everest expedition) could be squelched by an illness or injury *before I even arrived at base camp.* There is a constant, overriding fear of contracting a GI infection, spraining an ankle, or suffering some other minor injury that would be just enough to keep a climber from being at the top of his or her game. And not being at the top of your game may be just enough to keep you from getting to the top of the mountain. And if you make it to base camp in good health and then can manage to stay "relatively" healthy during the next six to seven weeks on the mountain (in spite of the altitude, the physical grind, the dicey food, and the sleep deprivation), then you just have to contend with the possibility that the weather, an equipment malfunction, an avalanche, or an accident along the route might thwart your efforts—or worse, kill you.

So yeah, when you're walking to base camp it's hard *not* to think about all the things that could go wrong during a high-altitude expedition, especially when you reach an area called Dugla Pass, where climbers and trekkers stop to pay respect to the fallen climbers whose lives were claimed by Everest and her neighboring peaks. No one remains unmoved upon reaching Dugla Pass. Dozens of cairns and chortens serve as memorials to those killed on Himalayan giants, a visual reminder that the mountain is always boss.

Many of the names engraved on the plaques or into the stones are familiar to those who know a bit about Everest's tragic history—for example, Scott Fischer's name is there.

Scott Fischer was one of the world's most experienced high-altitude climbers and was the owner of the adventure company Mountain Madness. He was one of eight people who died during a summit attempt on May 10–11, 1996. (The events surrounding his death were chronicled in Jon Krakauer's *Into Thin Air* and in Anatoli Boukreev's *The Climb.*) In total, fifteen people died that year on Everest, making it the deadliest season in Everest's history.

Other names, like that of British climber Peter Legate, are less well-known to most people but are painfully familiar to me. Peter was killed on April 30, 2002, when he slipped and fell more than six hundred feet down one of the steepest parts of the route, the Lhotse Face. My team was back at Camp 2 getting ready to make our way up the Lhotse Face to Camp 3 when the accident occurred. We heard Pete's climbing partners screaming for help, but nothing could be done. He died from the injuries he sustained during the fall.

These memorials serve as sobering reminders to all who pass through that area that sometimes no matter how skillful or strong or experienced you are, things can still go wrong. Lots of things.

———

After ten days of trekking through the Khumbu region, you finally reach base camp, which becomes home to several hundred climbers for a few months each year. And now it is *game on*. This is when it hits you: *I am about to climb Mount*

Everest. Base camp sits at an elevation of nearly 17,600 feet and is peppered with tents during the climbing season. This camp is luxurious compared to the other camps higher up on the mountain. Most climbers get their own tent, which provides some much-needed solitude throughout the climbing season. Teams typically also have a toilet tent, a shower tent, and a mess tent where everyone gets together. (Getting together happens only in the mess tent. You're on your own in the toilet tent and shower tent.) Almost every expedition employs a team of Sherpas at base camp that does the cooking and will even help with chores like washing clothes every now and then, if you so desire. There's a ton of support at base camp, so it feels relatively comfortable as compared to the other camps higher up on the mountain. I mean, it's not like the Sherpas leave mints on your pillow at night, but it's easy living compared to what you contend with as you begin your foray up the big white monster.

Once climbers reach base camp, they spend several days organizing gear and equipment and preparing for whatever the mountain might throw at them during the expedition. Last chance to sharpen the crampons and make sure everything is in working order while there is still access to supplies and tools, because once you get higher up on the mountain, Home Depot stores are hard to come by. And, perhaps most important, climbers participate in a *puja* ceremony before they begin their climb. A *puja* is a traditional Buddhist ceremony conducted at base camp by a lama who blesses all members of the climbing team and asks the gods to keep the team out of harm's way. A stone altar is built, and climbing equipment is laid at the base of the altar to be blessed during the ceremony. Prayer flags are affixed to a pole rising high above the altar, and these flags fly over base camp for the duration of the expedition to protect those on the mountain.

After spending several days at base camp getting used to the altitude, you're ready for action. It's now time to begin the actual climb, and this is where things really get serious because you have to cross through the most dangerous part of the route to get to Camp 1—the dreaded Khumbu Icefall. I'll go into more detail on the Icefall later in the book, but for now, suffice it to say that this Icefall is scary as hell because it's riddled with crevasses (huge chasms in the glacier that are sometimes hidden by snow) as well as massive ice blocks the size of small buildings that can come crashing down on you at any moment. Even diehard atheists have been known to mumble prayers under their breath while moving through the Icefall.

Assuming you make it to Camp 1, you generally spend the night there at an altitude of about 19,500 feet. This is where you really begin to feel like you are on an overwhelmingly enormous mountain, as Camp 1's elevation is just about eight hundred feet shy of the elevation of the summit of Alaska's Mount McKinley (20,320 feet)—the highest peak in North America. But you still have more than 9,000 feet of altitude gain ahead. It takes climbers an average of four to seven hours to get to Camp 1, so you're not in the mood for horseshoes and volleyball when you get there. Most climbers fall into their tents to rest and pretty much stay there until the next day. After a well-earned night of sleep, it's rise and shine—time to take on the mountain again. Onward, right? Well, not exactly.

This is where my point comes in with regard to having to go backward in order to make progress. After spending a night up at Camp 1, you get up and eat breakfast and pack up your gear and head *back down to base camp*—back through the Icefall, across the shaky ladders, over the crevasses. Once you are back at base camp you spend a few nights there again. More big meals in the dining tent, courtesy of your Sherpa staff. Maybe a little laundry gets done if you're really motivated. *Why come back down to base camp again?* you ask. Isn't that in the opposite direction of where you are trying to get to? Well, *yes*. But there's good reason for heading back down, and I could tell you now, but I'd rather keep you in suspense for a few more pages. Here's a hint: it's all related to physiology and the effects of altitude. Stay with me...I promise this is going somewhere.

After a few days of "comfort" at base camp it's back to work—back through the Icefall again as you head up the mountain. That's right—you climb to Camp 1 again. Déjà vu. Good to be back. After spending another night at Camp 1, the next day you climb up to Camp 2 (approximately 21,000 feet), which is situated on the Khumbu glacier at the base of the Western Cwm (pronounced "coom"—it's a Welsh word, in case you were wondering). While there isn't much elevation gain between Camps 1 and 2, the route is heavily crevassed, and climbers should be careful to clip into the safety lines along the glacier. Camp 2 is also known as Advanced Base Camp (or ABC) and has many more comforts than Camp 1. Usually teams have a communal mess tent for meals and some kind of crude toilet tent (at Camp 1 there is little cover, so modesty is something you leave at base camp).

Bear in mind that the weather can interrupt the scheduled flow of events at any time. The same goes for illness, fatigue, or accidents. But assuming everything is going smoothly (plenty of sunshine, no wind, no torn ligaments, and no explosive you-know-what), most teams will spend a night or two at Camp 2 and then the next day, sure enough, they head back to base camp *again*. Yeah, back *down*. So there you are. *Again*. Back down at 17,600 feet. More big meals in the dining tent, more relaxing in the thicker air at lower elevation, more time to repair gear or sew up the holes in your clothes that you've managed to tear. After a few more nights spent down at base camp, the teams then head back up the mountain for yet another rotation. Back through the Icefall yet again, up to Camp 1 (again), then Camp 2 (again), and then all the way up to Camp 3, which is about two-thirds of the way up the Lhotse Face.

Lhotse is another 8,000-meter peak that borders Tibet and Nepal and is adjacent to Mount Everest. It is the fourth-highest mountain in the world, with an elevation of 27,940 feet (8,516 meters). The southeast ridge route on Mount Everest requires ascending a good portion of Lhotse before you hang a hard left and cross over to the mountain you're actually trying to climb. The Lhotse Face is a steep, icy, 3,700-foot wall that requires fixed lines of rope to be anchored into the ice at various spots for safety. This section of the route can take climbers more than nine hours, because their bodies are not yet used to the altitude.

This will be the toughest day that climbers will endure up until summit day. Some people think it's even rougher than summit day, because you climb to Camp 3 at 24,000 feet without supplemental oxygen, whereas on summit day approximately 96 to 98 percent of all climbers use oxygen tanks during their push to the top. There is about 3,000 feet of altitude gain between Camp 2 and Camp 3, and the pitch is steep (40–50 degrees). The steepness is constant and the glacial ice is treacherous. The ice is so solid on this part of the route that even the most experienced climbers can't self-arrest, which is the process of stopping a fall by plunging your ice axe into the terrain below you (you can also self-arrest by using your hands, feet, knees, or whatever you can thrust into the terrain below you if the snow is soft enough—which is not the case on the Lhotse Face).

Camp 3 is the most uncomfortable camp. There are no flat areas to set up tents, so you have to dig out small platforms that are just large enough for the tent footprint. There is no room to walk around, and as a result there is not much socializing at Camp 3 other than speaking loudly enough from your tent so that whoever is in the tent a few feet away can hear you. Just stepping outside of your tent when nature calls can be a harrowing experience. There, you spend a very long, cold, restless night (and if you are me, you do not spend it in your sleeping bag but in the tent vestibule throwing up your last meal, thanks to the altitude). Then after a brutal night at Camp 3, guess where you go? Yep. *All the way back down to base camp, again.*

Okay, time to end the suspense and stop torturing you. So why do you have to keep coming back down to base camp again after climbing up to the higher camps on the mountain? Because of a process known as *acclimatization*, which is a fancy word for the process of adapting to high altitude. If someone were to magically drop you off at the summit of Mount Everest (pretend you could be dropped there by plane or helicopter or something like that), you would be dead in a matter of minutes from the sudden altitude gain, so you have to move up the mountain very slowly to let your body get used to the altitude.

Why is altitude stressful on the human body? Because it affects respiration, for starters. Altitude also shakes up your cognitive abilities and brain function. Motor skills, memory, reaction time, and mood are affected at very high elevations. But you don't have to be at 18,000 feet to feel the effects of altitude. If you've ever traveled directly from sea level to a ski resort mountain, you probably felt short of breath and maybe even developed a headache or a slight feeling of nausea. You may have chalked it up to the previous night's beer pong or tequila shots, but most likely it was due to the altitude. A mere 8,000 feet above sea level is considered "high altitude." Some people will feel the effects at that elevation and some won't—it varies for everyone.

People feel sick at altitude because the atmospheric pressure is lower. The percentage of oxygen in the air always remains constant at around 21 percent, but because there is less pressure at higher altitudes the oxygen molecules spread out, so you take in fewer molecules with every breath. The opposite is true for lower elevations—the atmospheric pressure is greater, so the weight of the air compresses the molecules, and you take in more oxygen with each breath. At 18,000 feet your body is getting 50 percent less oxygen than it would at sea level. During the acclimatization process more red blood cells are produced so that oxygen can be carried through the body more efficiently. In other words, your body learns to function with a smaller supply of oxygen. So while your mind may be ready to go higher up the mountain, your body needs time to adjust. Pushing this is a bad idea. If your body is not properly acclimatized, there is greater risk of developing altitude sickness, which is something you definitely want to avoid.

Altitude sickness can take many forms—Acute Mountain Sickness (AMS) presents in the form of a headache or nausea, which can be annoying at the least and debilitating in more severe cases. The real danger comes when AMS progresses to High Altitude Pulmonary Edema (HAPE), which is a buildup of fluid in the lungs, or High Altitude Cerebral Edema (HACE), a swelling of the brain. These forms of altitude sickness can be deadly. While headaches and nausea often subside, when signs of HAPE or HACE are present the climber must descend immediately, and descending still doesn't ensure the person will survive. This stuff is nothing to mess with. The best way to avoid altitude sickness is to ascend slowly in order to give your body time to adapt. But here's the catch: at altitudes above 18,000 feet, climbers experience insomnia, weight loss, and muscular weakening. That means the body is deteriorating at any elevation above base camp.

So while it is important to spend time up high on the mountain in order to facilitate the metabolic cell changes necessary to carry oxygen throughout your body, it's also important to spend time back down at a lower elevation in order to eat, sleep, hydrate, and regain some strength. It is indeed very physically challenging to be going up the mountain…then back down…then back up higher…then back down again. But psychologically it is incredibly frustrating as well, because you know you need to be going *up* in order to reach the top, but you spend a heck of a lot of time climbing *down*. What you have to remember is that even though you are physically moving away from your goal, you are in fact still making progress toward your goal because you're helping your body acclimatize.

Retreating to base camp's lower elevation is an important part of staying healthy throughout the climb so that climbers have the best possible shot at making the summit should the weather and other external factors cooperate. The body must go in the opposite direction in order to gain strength and reenergize—and this allows climbers to move faster and ascend higher the next time they head up the mountain. This is, by all means, moving toward the goal.

For whatever reason, we tend to think that progress has to move in one particular direction, but that's simply not the case. Sometimes you *do* have to go backward—away from your destination—in order to reach it. The mental trick is to understand that going down does not mean you're losing ground, but rather strengthening the foundation of your effort.

You shouldn't look at backtracking or starting over as a bad thing. It's just part of the normal climbing routine on big peaks, and it's something we have to do if we want to get better, stronger, and really stretch ourselves to achieve more. Yes, it's a drag and it can be mind-numbing at times, but rarely does anyone achieve anything worthwhile without dealing with some repetition and monotony. Think about the scientists working on the Human Genome Project. That work started in 1990 and took more than thirteen years before it was considered complete. You think those guys didn't have to go back to the drawing board a gazillion times before figuring out how to map DNA?

Even professional sports figures who are at the top of their game do the same drills over and over and over again, not because they haven't mastered the exercise, but because the repetition builds strength and enhances agility. When you see champion athletes on the court, on the field, or in the ring, keep in mind that they got there by focusing on the fundamentals—over and over again.

While retracing steps or going over something that is already familiar can feel like a burden, it's clearly not a waste of time. And going backward doesn't mean you are erasing progress. There is real value in going back to your starting point to regroup, to reenergize, and to reposition yourself to be stronger so you can ascend to the next level.

File under "Heading in the Right Direction"

Progress doesn't always look like progress and it doesn't always feel like progress. But no matter what it looks or feels like, anything that makes it more likely that you'll reach your goal is…progress. So look for examples of hidden progress in your life and work—and encourage others to do the same. Reward and encourage progress in all forms, not just the obvious ones.

Chapter 3

CHOOSING YOUR TEAM

Experience, Expertise, and Ego

On expeditions where teams face danger on a daily basis, climbers literally put their lives in their climbing partners' hands, so you better choose your team wisely. Recruiting mistakes can be costly. We're not talking about the difference between winning or losing market share—we're talking about life and death.

In extreme environments when everyone is feeling stress, there is no employee handbook you can reference to figure out how to deal with difficult people. Dr. Phil is not going to show up to counsel you on the proper way to handle people who aren't working well with others or are more concerned with themselves than they are with meeting team goals. That's why you must choose your partners wisely, be it in business, life, or sport.

I knew there was a lot at stake when I first started recruiting members for the first American Women's Everest

Expedition in 2002. I also knew I needed help, because at the time I just didn't know that many female climbers who would be both interested in and qualified for an Everest climb. I contacted everyone whom I had ever climbed with in the past and asked them to reach out to their networks in order to help me compile a list of names and climbing résumés. Naturally, I was immediately drawn to the women who had the beefiest climbing bios—women who had climbed the most mountains, the highest mountains, the toughest mountains. But I realized very quickly that it wouldn't do me any good to be high up on a mountain with the world's most elite climbers if they didn't care about the rest of the team. I also realized that I didn't want to be up there with people who were just fun and cool and easy to get along with if they lacked the necessary skills to survive and succeed in that environment. When you're taking on a big mountain, you have to find people who are the perfect mix of skill, experience, and desire. And not just the desire to climb, but the desire to be team players.

I wasn't looking for women who just wanted to scale Everest—I needed athletes on the team who would embrace the experience of climbing with other women and who would be proud to wear the American flag on their jackets. And then there was the question, *Would I trust this person with my life?* If the answer was "yes," then I had to ask myself, *Is this someone with whom I would want to spend two months in a tent?*

Our sponsor, the Ford Motor Company, set some other requirements for team members that knocked some fabulous women out of the running, but their recruiting guidelines made perfect sense to me. The team members had to be American, they had to be women (after all, it was the first American Women's Everest Expedition), and they could not be professional climbers. Ford didn't want the team to be comprised of professionals, because they were creating a PR campaign focused on sending a message about pushing your limits, challenging yourself, and getting outside of your comfort zone—which meant doing something that required you to stretch. Of course, climbing big mountains can be a stretch for professional climbers and full-time mountain guides, but it's something they get paid to do frequently. That was why Ford decided they wanted the team to be "regular women" who were strong mountaineers but who didn't do it for a living. Ford dubbed the project "Team No Boundaries," which went along with the "No Boundaries" ad campaign for their SUVs back in 2002. They wanted people to look at our team and say, "Hey, if those ladies are climbing Everest, then maybe I can [fill in the blank]."

There wasn't enough time or money to interview prospective teammates in person, so I had to decide who would make the final cut based solely on phone interviews (we didn't have Skype back then). But the process proved to be easier than I anticipated. It usually didn't take me more than a few minutes of conversation to know if I wanted the person on the other end of the line to join the team. It wasn't hard to tell which of them were going to be good team members and which might not be as good a fit. Some women asked questions like, "How much are we getting paid?" or "Are we flying first class?" "Nothing" and "No" were the answers to those questions. I worried that these women wouldn't be the best fit for our team, because they seemed more interested in money and perks than in the opportunity to be part of something really special—something that would happen only once in a lifetime. But other women asked questions like

"What can I do to help? Can I help raise funds for the trip?" or "Even if I am not selected to be a part of the team, can I pay my own way to base camp and cheer you on from there? Can I design a website for you? What can I do to be part of this team if I am not given a spot on the actual climb?"

This was precisely the kind of upbeat response I wanted to hear. *You're in!* Alfred Edmond Jr., the senior vice president and editor at large of *Black Enterprise*, once shared some advice with me on the subject of recruiting talent: "Screen for aptitude, then hire for attitude." Looking back on my recruiting process in 2002, I realize I was doing just that. I had pooled names of all the candidates who had the skills to climb a monstrous mountain, and then made my choice based on who had the best attitude.

Joining me in Nepal for the first American Women's Everest Expedition were Jody Thompson, Kim Clark, Lynn Prebble, and Midge Cross. Jody, Kim, and Lynn were from Colorado, and Midge was from central Washington. All were talented outdoor athletes. We ranged in age from thirty-five to fifty-eight. Our backgrounds were completely different, but the one thing we all had in common was a passion for climbing mountains. And while none of us were professional climbers, the five of us had more than one hundred years of cumulative climbing experience between us. Interestingly, all but one of us had overcome some type of health challenge. I have had a few heart surgeries and suffer from Raynaud's disease, Midge has diabetes and is a breast cancer survivor, Lynn has osteoporosis and exercise-induced asthma, and Jody had developed HELLP syndrome, a life-threatening condition that occurs during pregnancy, and nearly died in childbirth. Her son Hans had to be delivered three months early and weighed a mere 1.5 pounds.

Accepting a spot on the team meant Jody would be leaving Hans, then eleven months old, for eight weeks while she was in Nepal. She later said that it was one of the hardest decisions she ever had to make. The fact that she had a supportive husband, Mark, who said, "*Go!* I'll figure out how we'll manage back at home," is what pushed her over the fence. Mark, an attorney and also an avid climber, realized this was an incredible opportunity for Jody and didn't want her to miss out on the experience. (This is an example of someone who chose her life partner wisely.)

Ford brought our entire team together for the first time during a photo shoot in Breckenridge, Colorado, about a month before we left for Nepal. It was great to have the opportunity to finally meet everyone. Ford also sent out its PR team from Hill+Knowlton to spend a few days with us in order to manage the photo shoot and help us prepare for our upcoming media tour.

The Hill+Knowlton folks filled us in on what would be expected of us during our scheduled television appearances, which would take place in New York the week before we headed off to Everest. They helped us prepare by going over messaging and conducting mock interviews so we would be ready when we were actually live on camera. Talk about getting out of your comfort zone. We were probably more nervous about our upcoming television appearances than we were about the climb. We also spent a good portion of the weekend posing for photos for the PR campaign. We even staged a ladder crossing to look like the Khumbu Icefall. And of course we took photos with the then-new 2003 Ford Expedition, which, you should know, is the only full-size SUV with independent rear suspension and optional third-row power fold seats—or at least it was at the time. (Hey, gotta plug the sponsor!)

During those two days in Colorado the team seemed to have good chemistry, so that was reassuring. We got to know one another, and we spent a lot of time talking and laughing and sharing our excitement and our fears about the challenges that lay ahead for us in Nepal. But we were in a comfortable environment with all the amenities we were used to at home (running water, toilets, showers, good food, and a thermostat to control the indoor temperature). How would this team fare on the highest mountain in the world in some of the most extreme circumstances that human beings ever face? How would we do when it became painful and uncomfortable and our bodies were being pushed to their limits? People can put up with just about anything for two days. But we were looking at *two months* together. With all the uncontrollable factors you have to deal with on a big mountain, the last thing you want to have working against you is team dynamics.

So how'd it work out? Well, let me say this: If I had to pull together another team of women, I would pick the exact same ladies (plus a few others I have climbed with in recent years). Every woman on that team was truly thankful for the opportunity to be there and behaved accordingly. They got a free trip to Everest, courtesy of Ford, and they were incredibly grateful for that. I don't think there was a single day when someone didn't mention how lucky they felt just to be on the mountain.

From the very beginning this group felt like a team. Even before we got to base camp we talked about the expectations we needed to meet—for one another and for our sponsor. We approached everything from a team perspective. We climbed together, obviously, but even during the downtime on our rest days we spent time strategizing about how we were going to approach the various challenges that were awaiting us higher up on the mountain. At one point we even made a pact that on summit day, if one person needed to turn around before we reached the top, the entire team would turn around with her. We wanted to send a strong message about solidarity and the bond among us and that this was more important than the top of a mountain. Climbing is often known as a selfish sport, and we wanted to shatter that myth.

We actually ended up scrapping that plan, because despite our best intentions, that type of strategy could have been detrimental. We were afraid that it might cause someone to push herself further than she should—past her limits to the point where it could be dangerous—because she didn't want to be the one who made the whole team turn around. That's how people die on Everest—they push themselves so hard to get to the top, and then they have nothing left to get themselves back down. We didn't want that to happen to anyone on our team. So in a sense, changing our mind was another expression of our bond.

There was not one time during the expedition when we didn't get along, which is actually *very unusual.* When you're with people 24/7 in isolated, extreme environments, it's completely normal for people to grate on one another's nerves and for tension to arise among team members. But not on this trip. Everest climbers who read this may roll their eyes—*Aw, c'mon!*—but I am telling the truth here. There was virtually no conflict among our team members. I kept waiting for things to go south. It never happened. There were no divas. There were no selfish climbers. Now, that's not to say that there wasn't conflict with others—those *outside* of our immediate team. With a big expedition there are a lot of folks involved in addition to the climbing team (logistics managers, base camp managers, communications managers, guides, etc.). Conflict is, of course, a predictable component of group dynamics, and it can actually be healthy.

Conflict becomes dangerous only when it is unresolved. That's when it can be destructive. When you're in an extreme, isolated environment and people start behaving badly, you can't threaten others by telling them that they'll be written up and a note will be put in their permanent file. You have to find ways to minimize people's crappy behavior as well as the impact of that behavior—and you have to do it right away. That means bringing the conflict out into the open, where you have a shot at resolving it. Communication is key. It's essential to make sure that each team member knows that he or she is valued and that his or her opinion matters.

When I speak to various organizations about leadership and recount the details of the expedition—including my admiration for my team—I am often asked what made that team of women so great. I always used to respond with, "I don't know—there was just this magic chemistry among the five of us." I would tell people that the women were all very easy to get along with, low-maintenance, appreciative of the opportunity, and incredibly considerate of one another and of the other folks involved with the expedition. I kept telling people, "I just got really lucky with the team."

It wasn't until October 2012, more than ten years after the expedition, that I realized why it was that our team was so special. I was at Duke University for our annual board meeting of the Fuqua/Coach K Center on Leadership and Ethics. Coach K (full name: Mike Krzyzewski) has been the head men's basketball coach at Duke for more than three decades. He had recently come back from winning gold as the head coach of the United States men's national basketball team at the Olympic games in London. Over breakfast that morning he shared with us his process of choosing the players for the US team. He said that one of the things he looks for in players is *ego*. He wants them to have it, and plenty of it. I thought, *Huh??? You want ego? Doesn't that go against everything I've ever read or have been taught about the kinds of people who make good team members?*

Coach K went on to explain that when you are trying to put together a high-performing team, you want people who are good and who know they're good—because that gives them the confidence to know they can win. Coach K calls it *performance ego*. Of course his team included Kevin Durant, Kobe Bryant, and LeBron James—three of the best players the game has ever seen. They had every right to have big egos. After all, stats don't lie. Coach K said he absolutely hates the phrase "Leave your ego at the door." He wants his players to exude confidence and to be who they are; he *does not* want them to rein it in. "I don't want LeBron James to walk into a room and be a wuss," he told us. (Actually, I don't think Coach needs to worry about that.)

Having a strong ego doesn't mean you're disrespectful of others, because you can bet that Coach K wouldn't put up with that. He has a list of standards that he expects from all of his players, college or pro:

- Look each other in the eye.
- Tell each other the truth.
- Never be late.
- Don't complain.
- Have each other's backs.

Coach went on to tell us about the second type of ego he wants and needs in his players—and that's *team ego*. He wanted everyone playing for him to feel extreme pride in being part of Team USA, and they did. For everyone involved it was about the opportunity to represent their country on the court. It was about national pride, not individual pride. It was an opportunity to be part of something truly unique that would bring together the best in the sport from all over the world. No one got paid to play on the US basketball team. They played for two months in the summer, then rejoined their NBA teams in September for training camp prior to the regular season, which started in October. So during the summer they were away from loved ones, they were risking injury, they were not getting paid, and they were doing it for *the team*—the chance to be a part of something that was greater than the sum of its parts.

Climbing is a sport that is also filled with big egos. Prior to listening to Coach K, I used to think a big ego was a bad thing, but I was confusing ego with arrogance. Coach K's ideas about egos made perfect sense to me. If you're going to put together a team to take on a big mountain, you want people who have what it takes and who *know* they have what it takes. You want them to think they're great at what they do. You don't ever want to climb the Hillary Step (one of the most technically demanding parts of the route) behind someone who, at 28,740 feet, is thinking, *I don't really know if I have what it takes to do this*. People who hesitate on the route cause bottlenecks, and this is a serious issue up in the death zone. Anything that slows down climbers is dangerous, because it increases the chances that something will go wrong. Climbers need to keep moving in order to generate enough body heat and energy to keep their extremities and organs alive. You can suffer hypothermia, frostbite, or maybe something worse from standing around in the cold on an exposed section of the route. You can even run out of supplemental oxygen. When that happens, people can die.

You want people on your team who look at the toughest parts of the route and just *know* they can crush it. (I'm talking justified confidence; self-delusion is a whole different story.) You don't have to actually enjoy all the hard parts (there were plenty of spots on Everest that I didn't like), but you have to be good enough to get past them and you have to have confidence in your abilities to do so.

After thinking about Coach's words, I realized that what made our team great wasn't luck or some kind of crazy magic (as I had been telling people for ten years)—it was simply a matter of *ego*. Those women had *performance ego*; more important, they had *team ego*. They were grateful to be a part of the first American Women's Everest Expedition. They were constantly thanking me for giving them the opportunity to take part. They kept talking about how indebted they felt to Ford for funding the trip and making it possible for us. They realized that they were part of something really special. Like the US Olympic basketball team, we weren't getting paid for our efforts (we were actually taking a financial hit because we were each forgoing two months' salary). We were going to be away from loved ones for a long time (sixty days), and then, as soon as we returned, we had to go back to our old jobs and hit the ground running. (I was at my desk at 6:00 the morning after I returned from Nepal.)

But that unique sense of team ego eclipsed the concerns about any of those things because we were hugely proud to be on that mountain as a team of American women. Sending a message about pushing your limits and getting outside of your comfort zone resonated with us, and that further strengthened our bond. It helps to believe that your purpose and mission are meaningful. And while our Everest team did not make it to the summit in 2002—we missed it by just a couple hundred feet due to a storm—it was the biggest honor of my life to have had the opportunity to be part of that expedition. It wasn't about the summit. *It was about the team.*

Fast-forward to my 2010 Everest climb, which was a completely different type of experience in terms of team dynamics. I joined a group of eight other mountaineers, none of whom I knew. Our expedition was organized by Alpine Ascents International, an expedition company based in Seattle.

The owner of the company, Todd Burleson, has completed the Seven Summits twice and has led eight expeditions to Everest. He also received the David A. Sowles Memorial Award from the American Alpine Club for his heroic efforts to rescue other climbers on Everest in 1996. But beyond Todd's accomplishments as a climber, I've always been impressed with his commitment to providing the best possible service when it comes to organizing expeditions.

Alpine Ascents has a reputation as one of the best in the business. There are plenty of nightmare stories about logistics providers who cut corners everywhere they can, use shoddy gear, and make promises about what they will provide for an expedition, only to break them once they pocket your money. I have learned this the hard way on various mountains in the past. I have known Todd for years and trust him implicitly. Alpine Ascents was responsible for all the expedition logistics—getting our permits in order, getting our equipment to base camp, and hiring and organizing the Sherpa team, guides, and base camp staff, and they did an exceptional job.

I met the other people I would be climbing with for the first time at the Hotel Yak and Yeti in Kathmandu. The group ranged in age from twenty-one to sixty-five. While the demographics of the team were diverse, everyone had a strong climbing background. We were all there to accomplish the same thing—scale Mount Everest and come back alive—and while we were all climbing the mountain together at the same time, we did not always function as a team. But this was to be expected, because we weren't there as a team.

Well, what is a team, then? The *Merriam-Webster Dictionary* says a team is "a number of persons associated together in work or activity." I vehemently disagree. Just because you have a group of people doing the same thing at the same time—even if you have the same goal (like climbing a big peak)—it doesn't make you a team. It just makes you a group of people doing something at the same time. A group is only a team when every member of the group cares as much about helping the other members as they care about helping themselves.

While I definitely felt that every member of my 2002 team was working to help everyone else, I didn't feel that way about everyone I climbed with in 2010. That's not to say that I didn't like these people—I really did like them (well, most of them). There were some amazing climbers who were polite and considerate and helpful and selfless. Some of them were indeed *phenomenal teammates* with whom I stay in touch; I'd climb with them again anytime. But we were all there as individuals who wanted to climb the mountain for our own individual reasons.

We shared a base camp and guides and Sherpas and group gear, but we were all making our own decisions with regard to the climb. For example, each person could decide when he or she wanted to move up to the higher camps or when to retreat to lower elevations. And, of course, everyone had every right to focus on their individual needs, given that they didn't come there as part of a team. This was not unique to our group by any means—it is pretty much how most expeditions work. But it was an adjustment for me, because attempting to climb Everest as part of a group was different from taking on the mountain with an already-established team. An excerpt from my expedition journal illustrates this:

May 10, 2010. The team dynamics are proving to be as interesting and challenging as the mountain. After seven nights at Camp 2 and one night at Camp 3 (24,000 feet), I can tell you that the team that will finish this climb together will look very different than the team that started out together. A failed attempt on the Lhotse Face was what really started things on a bit of a downward spiral. We spent several nights at Camp 2 acclimatizing, and then at 5:00 a.m. on May 3rd we made our way up the steep face of hard blue ice. It was the most demanding part of the route and the toughest terrain we had encountered so far. About six hours into it we got hit with some pretty brutal weather and we had to abandon our attempt and return to Camp 2. We were only about 600 feet away from the Camp 3 tents when we turned, but the gusts of wind were so strong there was no way we could continue to move upward. It was incredibly demoralizing to be that far into the ascent to Camp 3 and have to turn back.

By the time we reached the safety of our tents back at Camp 2, the team was exhausted both mentally and physically. The weather was supposed to remain poor for the next two days—and we had already been delayed by weather for a few days at the beginning of this rotation, so rather than wait another two days and then make another attempt at reaching Camp 3, several people decided it would be better to go *back down* to base camp, where our bodies could recover at a lower altitude. The problem was that several other people decided the best thing to do would be to wait another two days and go fight our way back up that face that had just shut us down. There was discussing, there was reasoning, there was arguing, there was pissed-offedness. In the end, five of the climbers decided to pack up and go down to base camp the next morning, and four decided to stay up at Camp 2 and give that damn Lhotse Face another whirl. I stayed. I climbed. For nine hours I fought my way up that Lhotse Face and made it to Camp 3 along with Jackie, Victoria, and Jerry. Alpine Ascents guides Vern and Michael (Jackie's private guide) came up, too—and naturally our awesome Sirdar, Lakpa, was with us every step of the way.

Of course, I threw up in my tent vestibule that night (excellent)—but you don't get any extra points for that, as puking isn't all that unusual at nearly 24,000 feet. I was miserable all night, but I am *so* glad that I stayed with the group that went up to Camp 3. Climbing that Lhotse Face was a good confidence builder. *Plus*, those who did not go up with us are at a big disadvantage from an acclimatization standpoint, because now they will have to make a summit attempt after only having slept as high as Camp 2. Funny thing is that I *did* actually think about going back down to base camp with the others who abandoned the attempt, but my kneecap was so badly bruised from the day before (injured during our failed attempt on the Lhotse Face when I slammed it into the ice on a vertical pitch) that I didn't think I *could* get down, so that helped make up my mind to stay, take a rest day at Camp 2, and then try it again. Luck was with me this time.

We will sleep at base camp tonight and then head back down valley in order to let our bodies recover at a *lower* altitude. Yeah, we want to go lower than base camp to breathe some of that thicker air. Maybe my appetite will even come back. Oh, and FYI—of the five guys who came down from Camp 2 after giving up on climbing Lhotse to get to Camp 3, only two of them are still here at base camp. The other three were not feeling well and took a helicopter (dangerous at that altitude and $$$$!!!!) all the way back to Kathmandu, where they are relaxing at the Hyatt (perhaps the fanciest hotel in town) and are deciding whether or not they will continue on this expedition. I really hope that they do.

Thinking about them hanging out at a luxury hotel when the rest of us are here at base camp makes me realize that we are in different places not just physically, but also psychologically. Waking up and ordering room service, playing tennis, and sipping mai tais by the pool is quite a departure from base camp life. I hope the thick air and easy living helps them get healthy quickly so they can rejoin the climb. It would be a shame for anyone to quit this far into the expedition, although I know that illness is tough to recover from at high altitude, and each individual has to look out for their own best interests and do what feels right to them.

During one of the most critical parts of the climb, people scattered and divided into three groups. Some moved up to Camp 3, some retreated to base camp, and some chartered a helicopter to take them all the way back to the Hyatt in Kathmandu with a plan to come back to the mountain and rejoin the expedition after some R&R at sea level.

Everyone had a right to do what they did. There was nothing wrong with people deciding to go their separate ways. Again, this is how the majority of expeditions operate on Everest. It is what participants expect, and it's what most of them want. No one had any moral obligation to make decisions or take action based on what others wanted to do. It just happened to be very different from my previous experience, where we all climbed together as a team. I definitely missed that sense of team ego that we had back in 2002, when we locked arms from day one.

The feeling that our group was disconnected definitely hit me the hardest at the very end of the trip, when everyone was preparing to leave base camp for our journeys home. Our base camp manager came around to each of our tents and asked us about our plans to get back to Kathmandu. I was sort of confused at first when she asked the question, because I assumed everyone in our group was hiking out together—a trek that would take just a couple of days. (The trek out is much shorter than the usual ten-day trek in because everyone is acclimatized, and you're heading downhill into the thicker air, anyway.) She informed me that some people were opting to take a helicopter straight back to Kathmandu instead of making the trek back to Lukla and then flying to Kathmandu from there. I didn't realize that this was an exit strategy that many (probably most) climbers opt for after their expeditions. The helicopter ride is an attractive way out of the Khumbu for exhausted climbers who are anxious to get home to loved ones. I asked which climbers had reserved seats on the helicopter. She said, "So far...all of them."

A helicopter costs a few thousand dollars. The plan was that everyone who wanted to fly out would chip in and split the cost. I understood the rationale for wanting to leave on a helicopter—everyone wanted to get home as quickly as possible. People had families and kids and business to take care of. The expedition was over. They had mentally finished the climb, even if they were still on the mountain. Their work was done.

But getting on a helicopter and flying away from base camp didn't feel right to me. For one thing, it felt too abrupt. I wasn't psychologically ready to detach myself from the mountain. For all of its dangers, Everest was still a place I loved; a peak that had taught me so much—one with which I felt a deep connection. I wanted to try to draw things out and savor every last moment—even if it meant delaying access to a flush toilet. And, more important, I wanted to hike out with the people who had been so incredibly helpful for the past two months. If the base camp staff and Sherpas and guides had to walk out (and they did, given the price tag of a helicopter ride), then I wanted to walk out with them. I knew the reality was that I would probably never see most of them again, which depressed me. The posttrip blues were already sinking in, and the trip wasn't even over yet. Skipping the helicopter and spending a few days walking out instead was a way to put off the inevitable—the end of the trip and the sad good-byes.

Although I wasn't joining the other climbers for the helicopter ride back to Kathmandu, I wanted to spend as much time with them as I could before they all departed. Our assistant base camp manager, Joe Kluberton, and I joined them the next morning for their trek down to Gorak Shep, a tiny village about two hours down valley from base camp, where the helicopter would pick them up. I waited with everyone there until the helicopter arrived, all of their gear was loaded, and they were ready to take off.

A big round of hugs followed as we said our last farewells. I was nervous for them, because takeoffs and landings are tricky at high altitude (Gorak Shep is nearly 17,000 feet). Flying in the Himalayas requires some serious piloting skills. According to the Aviation Safety Network's database, close to seven hundred people have died in plane crashes in Nepal. As my friends took off, I held my breath and waited until they were completely out of sight before I let it out again, because everyone knows that if you hold your breath, it lessens the likelihood that anything bad can happen. After the helicopter vanished into the sky I let out a heavy sigh. They would be okay. So would I.

I spent the next couple of days hiking out with Joe and the rest of our base camp staff, guides, and some of our Sherpas. We got back to Kathmandu and celebrated our return to civilization in proper fashion—with a big fat steak dinner and a few rounds of cocktails. We met up with other teams that evening and hit the town in a big way. If I had to do it all over again I would choose to leave the expedition in the exact same fashion (but perhaps with fewer tequila shots during the farewell dinner).

When I got back to the States, I wasn't quite myself. I was feeling really blue and had trouble sleeping and didn't want to be social. I wasn't sure what was troubling me, really. I had just spent the entire spring on Mount Everest, and I had made some great friends. It was an awesome trip. The staff, guides, and Sherpas *more* than delivered—they could not have been any better at their jobs.

It took me several weeks to pinpoint what was wrong. I finally realized that although the expedition was a fantastic experience, I missed feeling that sense of *team ego* that we had felt in 2002. But of course, this expedition wasn't set up to be a team climb. It was set up so that whoever wanted to take a shot at getting up that big hill could do so in whatever style they were comfortable with. I was fortunate to have been with a group of (mostly) fabulous people during the two months we were on that mountain in the spring of 2010. I was impressed with the way many of them helped out when times got tough (and some went above and beyond the call of duty, for sure). But the reality was that most of them were there to accomplish something on their own.

There is a unique and extraordinary magic that comes with working your tail off and accomplishing something as a team. During our 2010 expedition, some of us worked together as a team—and that was amazing and enjoyable, and I am so grateful to those who did. But the group as a whole did not have that overall sense of team ego, and as a result I felt sort of empty when I got home.

Coach K nailed it that morning during our meeting when he said, "If you try to win alone and you're successful, you're going to jump up to celebrate alone. No one will share the moment with you. If you win as a team, you'll all jump up together."

I realize that telling you to encourage your people to have strong egos is a contrarian approach when it comes to forming a cohesive, high-performing team. But it worked for my 2002 Everest team, and it can work for you. Don't take it from me; take it from Coach K, who happens to be the winningest Division I men's college basketball coach in history. And oh, by the way…in addition to his unparalleled success as a college coach, he has coached sixty-three games for the USA men's national basketball team. His record? 62–1. He lost only one game—to Greece in 2006 during the semifinals of the World Championship. He said it was the worst loss he has ever endured as a coach. I remember watching that game on television. It still haunts me every time I eat feta cheese.

File under "Teamwork"

Timing, proximity, and a common goal are not enough to form a cohesive team. Teamwork is about looking out for one another, helping one another, and winning together. And if you are lucky enough to be in a position where you have some say in choosing your team, look for the Three Es: experience, expertise, and ego.

Chapter 4

FRIENDS IN HIGH PLACES

Get Your Network On

The legal disclaimer that is always attached to financial investment offerings should also be thought of as directly applicable to mountaineering: *"Past performance is not necessarily indicative of future results."* You can have five great climbs on the same mountain, but that doesn't ensure that your sixth is going to be as smooth; there are too many variables that you cannot control. Even if a landscape appears familiar from past expeditions, there will always be elements of unpredictability. Plenty of incredibly accomplished and experienced mountaineers end up in trouble—or even die—on routes they may have climbed multiple times.

Bad things happen to good climbers. Of course bad things happen to bad climbers, too, and much more often. But my point is that even if you're 100 percent confident in your team's skills and have a strong performance record, you may still find yourself in situations where you need help. Sometimes, no matter how good you are or how experienced you are, things can still go wrong. That's why it's good to have people around who you can count on to help you out when or if you are in a dire situation. Because sometimes, when you least expect it, you need to call for backup.

Some of the most talented climbers I know have gotten themselves into terrible jams in the mountains. I have a friend who is a top-notch endurance athlete and has summited multiple 8,000-meter peaks in the Himalayas; he had to be rescued from 13,700 feet on Mount Rainier (which tops out at 14,410 feet) in Washington State after two members on his rope team slipped and fell into a crevasse, yanking the entire rope team down with them. He fractured eight vertebrae and busted a wrist, an ankle, and a fibula. He was an incredibly strong climber, knew the mountain well, and had climbed it in the past. The injuries he and his climbing companions sustained were bad enough. Even worse, a young park ranger fell to his death while trying to rescue the stranded climbers, a tragedy that all involved will forever mourn.

The National Park Service employs climbing rangers on many mountains in the United States whose jobs include search-and-rescue operations. But you can't rely on that kind of help on most big peaks outside of the United States; there is no organization tasked with aiding climbers along the route. That makes it even more important to put real time and effort into building relationships and forming partnerships during expeditions. And I don't mean with just the people on your team. You have to be really strategic and think about extending your social network to those outside of your group.

One of the first things I do when I arrive at base camp on any mountain is walk around and talk to members of the other teams. I like to drop in on all the various campsites to say hello and meet the other climbers whom I will inevitably run into on the route. People often tease me about being overly social, but while I like meeting new friends, I'm not making the rounds in hope of winning the Miss Congeniality title. I do it because if, God forbid, something happens to someone on my team high up on one of those peaks, I want the climbers on the other teams to feel emotionally obligated to help us. You've probably heard the stories of folks who just walk right on by a dying or an injured climber on summit day. It should never happen…but the reality is that it does happen. You reduce your chances of being passed by when you have strong relationships in place.

Other teams can be tremendously helpful when things go wrong. And guess what? You may need to rely on other teams to make sure things go right. Rarely does one team operate independently of others within the same organization. Research and development, supply chain, engineering, manufacturing, quality control, sales and marketing—teams from each operational unit typically rely on one another to achieve certain milestones. The same is true for expedition teams.

Every spring dozens of teams arrive at Everest base camp, all with aspirations of tagging the tippy-top of the world's highest peak. Although these teams climb independently of one another, collaboration on the mountain is vital to ensure a safe and successful climbing season. For example, several parts of the route need to be "fixed" before climbers can ascend. "Fixing the route" refers to putting in the miles of nylon rope (known as fixed lines) that are anchored and left in place along the route so climbers can move along the steeper, more exposed sections of the mountain more quickly and safely. The fixed lines and ladders along the lower part of the mountain—those that run through the Khumbu Icefall and from Camp 1 to Camp 2—are set up and maintained throughout the season by a team of Sherpas called the Icefall Doctors (I feel a reality television show idea coming on...), but the upper portion of the route must be fixed by the climbing teams. This means that a person or a group has to climb all the way to the summit with the ropes and anchors (carabiners, snow pickets, ice screws) and set everything up for the masses of climbers who will eventually be making their way to the upper flanks of the mountain. Someone has to come up with the miles of rope, the anchors, the labor, and the oxygen required to get the job done. And someone has to pay for it all.

So, with no governing body at Everest base camp, who's in charge of getting the route fixed? Who is going to put up the resources? Who is footing the bill for everything? There is no matrix reporting structure and no designated project manager to oversee the process. This is where the true collaboration among teams comes in. The various expedition team leaders meet at base camp to sort it all out. Typically, a handful of teams donate the supplies and the financial and human resources needed to set up the ropes on the upper portion of the mountain. Sometimes the route-fixing meetings go smoothly, and other times there's a lot of controversy and complaining, maybe even some shouting and flared tempers. But ultimately the job gets done so that when the timing is right, climbers can go for the summit with a better shot at making it all the way up and back down as safely as possible.

Of course getting the timing right for a summit bid is always a challenge, as good weather windows are few and far between. The jet stream hovers over Everest's summit much of the year, and the winds up there can reach speeds of 175 miles per hour. Ideally, you want to go for the summit when the wind speed is below 30 miles per hour. That means you have to wait for the jet stream to move out, which usually happens during the month of May. But you can't wait too long, because the weather patterns change and the monsoons hit in June. It's tricky—which is why different teams subscribe to different weather forecasting services and share the information with one another. That data pooling can significantly help you identify the best times to climb.

Teams also try to coordinate the timing of their respective summit attempts to avoid crowds on the route. Naturally, everyone wants to take a shot at the top on the better weather days. But the results of overcrowding on the route can be tragic (and I'll get into more detail on this in the next chapter). Bottlenecks form at the more technical sections of the route, and as I mentioned earlier, climbers can get frostbite or run out of oxygen standing around waiting for the fixed lines to clear.

So do you bypass a good weather window to avoid the crowds and then hope another window opens up in a few days or weeks? What if another window doesn't open? What if the guys forecasting the weather got it wrong? What if everyone waits out the first good weather window, and as a result the route is too crowded during the second window? What if you decide to go for it now and burn through your bottled oxygen getting partway to the top, only to have the weather turn bad—and there isn't enough oxygen left to make another attempt? These are the kinds of scenarios you need to weigh, and your chances of making the right decision depend in large part upon communicating with other teams.

Team leaders—the smart ones, anyway—talk to one

another. They kick around ideas and come up with solutions that take into account that their respective teams are not alone on the mountain. Ultimately, they try to come up with a joint plan that makes the most of the weather windows and minimizes crowding on the route so that everyone has the best possible shot at success.

Collaboration among team leaders and base camp managers certainly leads to increased safety and efficiency on the mountain, but the networking and relationship building should not stop there. Every member of every team needs to reach across team boundaries. It needs to go deeper, down to an individual level. The team leaders play a vital part in helping manage what goes on among teams, but they may or may not actually be climbing the mountain. Many of them remain at base camp, equipped with a telescope and radio, and manage expedition logistics from there throughout the climbing season. Your base camp manager or team leaders may be the best networked people on the mountain, but if they aren't climbing with you, which is often the case, then their connections may not be enough to pull you through when you get up high.

Whether you're climbing a real mountain or a metaphorical one, you need to be proactive about forming your own partnerships. Don't leave the relationship building to others. Be strategic. Think about who you may need to call on for help at some point, and make sure you have relationships in place *before* you need the help. Even if you're not the most outgoing person in the world, you need to get your network on. Building relationships and forming partnerships can't physically get you to the top of a big peak (nothing can substitute for legs, lungs, determination, and warm underwear). But those abilities may mean the difference between living and dying.

Rarely has a single death on Everest captured as much media attention as the death of thirty-four-year-old British climber David Sharp in 2006, a tragedy that still stirs controversy today. Sharp, a math teacher from England, was climbing Everest for the third time after two unsuccessful attempts to reach the summit. He was climbing on a permit issued by Asian Trekking, a Nepali guiding company based in Kathmandu. But he was climbing alone, with no Sherpa support and no radio. He died, presumably on his way down from the summit.

The death of a climber on Everest isn't in itself hugely newsworthy. Incredibly heart-wrenching, but not out of the ordinary, as there are multiple deaths on Everest every year. Sharp's death became a high-profile story in the media because Discovery Channel was filming a reality TV series called *Everest: Beyond the Limit*, which followed a team from Himalayan Experience (Himex) as they climbed the Northeast Ridge route. Much of the filming was done via helmet cams worn by Sherpas along the route, so the footage literally took viewers along the entire journey of the climb. During the Himex group's summit bid, many of the climbers came upon Sharp sitting in a rock alcove at more than 27,500 feet between Camp 4 and the summit. The alcove, known as Green Boots Cave, is the final resting place of Indian climber Tsewang Paljor, who died in 1996. Paljor's corpse lies there, frozen into the terrain, with his green mountaineering boots clearly visible in the snow.

Dozens of climbers from various teams passed Sharp on their way to and from the summit. Some of them were aware that he was in trouble and some were not.

The footage aired during the series' first season. Many people who watched the program on the Discovery Channel or read about the events in the comfort of their homes were outraged. And while there were dozens of climbers high on the route that day, the Himex team took the most heat—in large part because they were the ones who were seen on camera heading up and down from the summit during the time that Sharp lay dying.

There is no question that this incident is one of the most controversial, disturbing, and heartbreaking events that has ever been reported on that mountain. The various teams whose members saw Sharp and kept moving all provided differing accounts of what happened. Many thought he was just sitting there taking a rest break and didn't realize that he needed help. Others mistook his motionless body for Paljor's corpse, which at that point had been in that cave for ten years. Some people did try to lend assistance, but they concluded that Sharp was so close to death that it would be impossible to save him.

The person most caught up in the David Sharp controversy was Himex owner/operator Russell Brice, a New Zealander who is a veteran Himalayan climber and has more than fourteen summits of 8,000-meter peaks, including two of Everest. Brice has been guiding for decades and is known for his strong opinions and direct style. He was the team leader of the Himex expedition, and he found himself smack in the middle of the debate about Sharp. Many who followed the media stories accused him of not doing enough to try to save Sharp's life.

But Brice wasn't anywhere near Sharp at the time of the incident. He was stationed back at the North Col (23,000 feet), monitoring his climbers' progress through a telescope and via radio. A segment of the Discovery program showed Brice instructing one of his climbers, Max Chaya, who came across Sharp on his way back from the summit, to leave Sharp and continue descending, believing that nothing could be done at that point. What the program did not show was that Brice sent one of his stronger Sherpas back up to the alcove with a bottle of oxygen to try to help Sharp, but his efforts proved fruitless as Sharp could not be revived.

People watching season one of *Everest: Beyond the Limit* did not see all the footage that was shot—only edited portions—so they did not have all the facts behind Brice's decision. Brice believed that because Sharp had been up in the death zone for so long without supplemental oxygen and was not mobile, he could not be saved or was perhaps already dead. There was a good chance that staging a rescue attempt would end in the deaths of more than one climber.

Many members of Brice's team were already in bad shape due to the exceedingly cold conditions that night coupled with the effects of high altitude and exhaustion. A number of them suffered frostbite as the temperatures dropped to fifty below. Mark Inglis, a double amputee who also came under fire for not helping Sharp, made the summit but was unable to descend on his own and had to be helped down the mountain. He later had to undergo further amputation to the stumps of his legs as well as to several fingers.

Generally speaking, climbers should try to help one another in the mountains. When you come upon a climber in trouble, you should drop your summit ambitions and try to help. That seems obvious. If someone's life can indeed be saved, then all climbers who are physically able to help absolutely have a moral obligation to attempt to save a life. No one would ever argue that. But "the right thing to do" isn't always obvious, because each set of circumstances is unique. And the harsh reality is that not everyone can be saved—which is tough stuff to chew on, for sure. In my view, Brice's first responsibility was to get all his people back down alive. He made a difficult decision—but not a callous or uncaring one.

Everyone seemed to have an opinion about the events surrounding David Sharp's death: the climbing community, those outside of the climbing community, the media, and so on. Sir Edmund Hillary, the first man to summit Everest, was quick to share his thoughts at the time: "I think the whole attitude towards climbing Mount Everest has become rather horrifying. The people just want to get to the top.... They don't give a damn for anybody else who may be in distress, and it doesn't impress me at all that they leave someone lying under a rock to die."

Was all the criticism warranted? I don't know. And neither do you, *unless you were there*. It's easy to be critical of other climbers from the comfort of your living room sofa. I especially remember one blogger's comments that read, "I have been to 23,000 feet and I can tell you that there is no doubt that I would have stopped to save him." There is a *huge* difference between 23,000 feet and 27,000 feet. And even if you've climbed into the death zone in the past and have stood on the very spot where Sharp died, you have no way of knowing exactly what went down unless you were there *at the time*.

Brice has taken part in more than fifteen high-altitude rescues. And while Sharp was not part of the Himex team, Brice retrieved Sharp's belongings and personally delivered them to his parents. This fact was not reported by most media outlets.

Sharp's parents understood that their son had made grave errors in judgment during his final attempt to climb Everest.

He was climbing alone and wasn't carrying a radio, which is hard to understand. Had he been carrying a radio, he may have been able to notify someone that he was in trouble.

He certainly had as much, if not more, experience than most successful summiteers on the mountain. He had previously summited Cho Oyu, a neighboring 8,000-meter peak in Nepal, so he knew what it was like to be in the death zone, where your lungs are screaming for oxygen while your body metabolizes itself in order to feed off its own tissue. This was his third attempt to reach the summit of Everest. The terrain was familiar to him. He knew what was required physically and psychologically. And in fact, 2006 was the year he finally made it. Unfortunately, he ran out of energy and oxygen and froze to death before he could make it back down.

Fast-forward to 2012, one of Everest's deadliest seasons. Ten people lost their lives on the mountain that year. But amid the media reports of the tragic deaths, there were also some inspiring stories of heroism. One of the most memorable had to be the rescue of forty-six-year-old Turkish American climber Aydin Irmak, who immigrated to the United States from Turkey in 1990. Irmak had little climbing experience. Despite what the media reports imply, most people who attempt to climb Everest have quite a bit of experience. There are often a few who show up ill-equipped and underexperienced; those people are exceptions to the rule. But Irmak happened to be one of those people. What was perhaps more concerning than his lack of climbing experience was his desire to pull off a unique stunt—he wanted to carry his bicycle to the summit. That, of course, required a permit from the ministry of tourism in Nepal, and they wouldn't allow it. (Score one for the Nepalese.) Still, he carried his bike partway to base camp, so most climbers were questioning his judgment (and sanity) from the time he arrived on the mountain.

Against all odds, Irmak did manage to climb to the summit. But the top of the mountain is only the climb's halfway mark—because you still have to get yourself all the way back down to base camp safely. Irmak couldn't do that; he began his descent and collapsed less than 1,000 feet below the summit, out of energy and out of oxygen—two things he desperately needed to make it back to the comfort of his tiny tent.

But Irmak got the lucky break of a lifetime when twenty-four-year-old Israeli climber Nadav Ben Yehuda, who was on his way up to the summit, happened to come upon him. Ben Yehuda saw a climber in distress—he did not realize who it was at first, but once he got closer he realized this was not just any climber. He shouted two words: "My brother!" The two men had befriended each other at base camp and formed a strong bond. There was absolutely no way Ben Yehuda was going to leave Irmak there to die. He abandoned his summit bid, and along with some Sherpas managed to help Irmak back down the mountain. Both men suffered frostbite and were eventually evacuated from Camp 2 by helicopter and taken to a hospital. Irmak would live to see another day and would have another opportunity to ride his beloved bicycle, thanks to the generous spirit of one man who didn't think twice about giving up his summit dream in order to save a life.

Keep in mind that many variables factor into whether or not someone will be rescued—where they are on the mountain at the time they collapse, the weather, the amount of time they have been without oxygen above 8,000 meters, how severe their condition appears to be (are they too far gone to save?), whether they are at all mobile, the strength and condition of the people who will be mounting the rescue attempt, and the stability of the terrain, among other things. But there's another factor, often overlooked: whether the people on the route actually know the distressed climber. People are more willing to risk their lives and well-being for people they know. In Irmak's case, Ben Yehuda felt a moral obligation to help because he considered Irmak a brother—even though they had met only a few weeks before. The fact that Irmak had relationships with others on the mountain saved his life.

To further illustrate the point about the importance of networking, check out these two quotations. One is from Ben Yehuda, the friend who rescued Irmak, and the other is from Mark Woodward, one of the Himex guides who was on Everest in 2006 at the time David Sharp was dying.

From a May 25, 2012, Associated Press article:

Ben Yehuda, who spoke to the AP just before leaving Nepal for urgent medical treatment in Israel, said he could not say with certainty how he would have reacted if he had come across a stricken climber he did not know. Oxygen is in such short supply and the conditions are so harsh, he said, that people on the mountain develop a kind of tunnel vision.

Ben Yehuda's honesty in that interview is to be admired. Everyone wants to think that they would do the right thing, the honorable thing, and help a struggling climber who would otherwise die if left to battle for his or her own life. But the fact is that when you are in the death zone, what seems plausible at lower elevations is not always possible. What you like to think you would do and what you are actually able to do are often different. Your brain is suffering from hypoxia and you can't always process information clearly or accurately. Some people have been known to hallucinate; others fail to notice events unfolding right in front of them.

One thing is certain: the fact that Aydin Irmak and Nadav Ben Yehuda got to know each other at base camp at the beginning of the climbing season and struck up a friendship altered the future for both climbers. Irmak got to live. Ben Yehuda did not get his shot at the summit but became a national hero at age twenty-four and received an award for his humanitarian efforts from Israeli president Shimon Peres. Lots of people climb Mount Everest. Not too many people receive presidential recognition and are categorized as heroes.

Now consider what Himex guide Mark Woodward said about David Sharp's death on Everest. This quotation appeared in an article from the August 2006 issue of *Men's Journal*:

We were kind of shining our head torches on him [Sharp] and going, "Hello, hello."...He didn't have any oxygen on him, and he had fairly thin gloves on. He was completely unresponsive and pretty well into a hypothermic coma, really. I realized that, you know, it was so cold that there was little chance that he would survive anyway. And primarily my responsibility is to the clients and people that I'm with. So at that stage, not knowing who he was or anything, I presumed that somebody from his expedition would be trying to do something if they knew he was still on the mountain.

Woodward made the best decision he could given the information he had at the time. Would things have turned out differently for Sharp had people known who he was? Would others have made more of an effort to help?

Maybe so. No one can know for sure what would have happened, but I can tell you that people will always be more inclined to help people they know as opposed to people they don't know. Responsible climbers are well aware of the risks involved when they decide to take on a mountain and will do everything in their power to position themselves for success (which means coming back alive). You just can't assume people you don't know will come to your rescue. You can pray for it, but you can't count on it, so that's why it's important to put effort into getting to know people and fostering relationships.

Maybe you won't ever be in a situation where networking is going to save your life, but it could very well change the course of your life. If it were not for some heavy-duty networking I would never have had the opportunity to climb the Seven Summits and ski to both Poles. My participation in each of those expeditions came as a result of others helping me to get to those places.

Take the first American Women's Everest Expedition in 2002. There is no way I could have raised the money and put together the team had I not spent time fostering relationships with classmates, friends, and people in the climbing community who made the trip a reality for me.

Here's how it went down: By 2001 I had climbed the highest peak on each of six continents and had done a lot of other climbing on lesser known but more difficult mountains. While expedition life fed my soul, I figured my passion for the outdoors had to be put on hold. I was fresh out of graduate school with $60,000 of debt from my student loans as well as $10,000 of credit-card debt that I had racked up during school. (Save it, Suze Orman.... We don't need to go there.)

Somehow, through luck and probably a lapse in judgment on the recruiter's part, I managed to land a job with Goldman Sachs upon graduation, which was one of the jobs most coveted by business school graduates. Now, most people think if you work at Goldman you're setting yourself up to make hundreds of thousands, if not millions of dollars each year. Some do score big at the firm, but only after they've been there a while or were hired away from another firm to fill a very senior position.

I, however, didn't fit either category. I was a very junior employee and was only there for three years and never made more than five figures. No, that wasn't a typo. Five figures. Don't get me wrong—I am *not* complaining by any means. I made a very respectable salary that I was grateful for—and it was more money than I had ever imagined making in my life. But I was living in San Francisco (one of the most expensive cities in the country, where parking costs more than monthly rent in most other towns) with $70,000 worth of debt. So, after paycheck deductions for medical coverage and taxes, I wasn't exactly living large. Given I wasn't making much of a dent in paying off my debt, an Everest expedition seemed completely out of reach. It was something that was not even on the radar, because I couldn't afford even the $30,000 price tag for one person to climb the mountain, let alone come up with the money for the entire team. It would never happen.

Then, in the summer of 2001 I got an e-mail that gave me a glimmer of hope and turned Everest from "never going to happen" to "maybe, possibly, long shot, but don't get your hopes up yet." A couple of women I knew had been throwing around the idea of putting together the first American Women's Everest Expedition, and they asked me if I would serve as team captain.

Ugh! I didn't feel ready to take on that kind of responsibility. I wasn't ready physically *or* psychologically. The whole thing felt intimidating beyond belief—too much of a stretch for me. In a nutshell, I was *scared*. And beyond my own hesitations about whether I was ready to take on a mountain like Everest (especially as the team captain), we had no way to fund the trip. None of the other women had any kind of budget for an expedition, big or small, either.

Several weeks later came the horrific events of September 11, 2001, which made me reconsider. Tragedies have a way of changing people's priorities and outlooks. As I watched the Twin Towers crumble on television, I thought about how life can change in an instant, and we don't ever really know what is waiting around the corner. September 11 was a wake-up call that gave me a sense of strength and resolve, and I realized that I needed to pursue the things I was passionate about. Even if those things were out of my comfort zone.

There are times in your life when you just have to *step up*—even if you feel like you aren't ready. This was one of those times. I decided that I was not going to let fear, nor a lack of funds, stop me from pulling this women's Everest team together. Getting over the fear was an internal battle I would have with my psyche, and I knew I could wage war and win. Getting the money was an entirely different challenge. I knew I needed to land some kind of corporate sponsorship. I have always felt that if you don't have money to do something you are passionate about, you *can* find the money if you are willing to put in the time. I had been granted permission to take a two-month unpaid leave of absence from work in order to climb Mount Everest, and I was going. That was that.

I started calling major corporations with deep enough pockets to come up with the kind of money we needed to send a team to the mountain. My efforts were discouraging, to say the least. Rarely were my phone calls or e-mails or letters returned. I was frustrated and disheartened from the lack of response. I knew I needed to get creative given the lack of love I was feeling from the prospects I had been approaching. I finally came up with a plan: instead of sending pitch e-mails and letters to companies, I started sending out the letters in a cardboard box, along with one of my hiking boots. I put the letter and the boot into the box, and at the end of each letter I closed with something like, "Whether or not you choose to sponsor our expedition, please send my boot back to me so I can keep training for the climb." I also enclosed a return FedEx label to make it easy for the recipient to send back my boot. Obviously I had another pair of hiking boots at home, so my training did not come to a halt while the boot was floating around. But sending my boot to prospects created a sense of urgency and forced them to take action since they needed to send the boot back to me. A little hokey—yes. But it worked! Well, sort of...

I sent my hiking boot to companies like Nike and other outdoor apparel manufacturers. I sent it to ESPN and other media outlets that I thought might be able to help. The new approach proved effective, and people actually started responding to my inquiries! People could ignore a letter or an e-mail, but they couldn't ignore my boot. The return package with my boot was coming back to me every few days; people were responding pretty quickly, since they knew I needed it back. The problem, though, was that they still weren't sending me checks. They were simply returning my hiking boot and letting me down easy by sending me notes of encouragement and moral support. And while I truly appreciated the black-and-white autographed glossy of Dick Vitale, it wasn't going to buy me an Everest climbing permit.

Finally, one day when I was at the pumpkin festival in Half Moon Bay (about thirty miles south of San Francisco) with some friends, we were walking the festival grounds sampling pumpkin dishes and looking at pumpkin displays when we came upon a display that stopped us in our tracks: not a pumpkin arrangement, but an automobile. And not just any old, ordinary automobile—it was a concept car and it was an impressive sight! It was a massive vehicle with tires that seemed to dwarf me in size. It was majestic and intimidating and gorgeous all at the same time. The white paint sparkled in the sunlight and seemed to be winking at me. For the sake of the environmentalists reading this I wish I could say this concept car was a Prius. But alas...it was a Ford SUV and it had a monstrous sign in front of it bearing the name *Himalayan Expedition*. Lightbulb. *Ford Ford Ford!!!! Ford should sponsor our expedition!!!*

I needed a way to get to the right people at Ford. And it just so happened that I had a business school classmate, Kevin Ropp, who worked in the Mercury division of Ford in Southern California.

I e-mailed Kevin a copy of our proposal, which outlined what we wanted to accomplish with the expedition and the funding we needed to make it all happen. Kevin reviewed our proposal and liked what he read. He mentioned that Ford's global director of marketing was a woman, and he thought she would be interested in what we wanted to accomplish as a team of female mountaineers. He promised me that he would do everything he could to help us. He started by forwarding the information up the ladder to the senior execs in Dearborn, Michigan.

While I was new to the process of fund-raising, I knew from my business experience that no deal is a done deal until the check is in hand, so while I was waiting to hear back from my pal Kevin I continued to network and pitch other companies in case Ford turned us down.

Then...finally...bingo! Kevin came through. He got the information to the right people at Ford. The Ford team then looped their advertising agency, J. Walter Thompson, in on the idea, and within a few weeks—after much negotiating—the deal was done. Our trip would be funded, and five American women would get to take a shot at the world's highest peak. *Thank you, Ford.* I will forever be grateful to that company.

It took a lot of work to close my first corporate sponsorship deal. I definitely had to cast a wide net and had to pitch dozens and dozens of companies in order to get anyone to even respond to me. I got a lot of rejections, of course, but all I needed was for *one* organization to come through. A lot of companies liked the idea but didn't have the funds. Others were excited about partnering with me but were worried about the liability. Mostly I hit roadblocks because I wasn't getting through to the right people. In the end, I took advantage (in a good sense!) of my relationship with Kevin Ropp, who took advantage of *his* relationships with coworkers who could get our proposal in front of the decision makers at Ford.

I also realize that much of the success in putting the deal together had to do with timing. Ford agreed to sponsor us because our expedition happened to coincide with the launch of their new full-size SUV—the 2003 Ford Expedition. What could be more perfect?!? It was our expedition paired with their Expedition—a match made in heaven.

I was absolutely thrilled that things worked out with Ford. Not just because it meant we were going to Everest, but because one of the other companies I was negotiating with at the time was Chevy, and their full-size SUV is the *Avalanche*. I'm no marketing genius, but I'm fairly certain that if you're going to Everest, it's much better to be sponsored by the Expedition than the Avalanche. Call me crazy....

File under "Relationships and Networking"

Developing strong relationships is critical to success, not only in the mountains but in just about any environment. It is especially important for leaders to connect with the right people. And when I say the "right people," I don't mean rich people or famous people or people in positions of power or influence. I'm talking about taking the time and making the effort to connect with people at every stage of your career, people who will rally around you, encourage you, and support you. And maybe even save your life—you never know.

Chapter 5

COMPLACENCY WILL KILL YOU

Make Your Move

In 1970, a Japanese extreme skier, thirty-seven-year-old Yuichiro Miura, became the first person to ski down Mount Everest.

He descended 4,200 vertical feet in 140 seconds. He had a parachute strapped to his back, which he was hoping would slow his speed to a manageable level. It didn't. Miura slid, tumbled, lost a ski, and miraculously came to a halt just a few hundred feet before the edge of a crevasse.

He may not have done it in the style he had hoped—but hell, he did it. He set a world record and he lived to tell. The film about his adventure, *The Man Who Skied Down Everest*, earned an Academy Award for best documentary feature and was the first sports film to do so. Miura is one of the most impressive extreme athletes in the world. Not only was he the first person to ski at an altitude above 26,000 feet; he also later went back to summit Everest. *Multiple times.* The first time at age seventy. The second at age seventy-five. But hold on, I'm not done: on May 23, 2013—at age eighty— Miura once again stood on Everest's summit and set a world record as the oldest person to do so. No, I'm not kidding. So the next time Grandpa says he's too tired to throw a ball around with his grandkids in the backyard, remind him of Yuichiro Miura.

The 1970 Japanese Everest Ski Expedition that made Miura an international sensation went down in the history books for more than just his incredible feat. It was also one of the most tragic Everest expeditions, as six Sherpas were killed in an avalanche in the Khumbu Icefall. It was the worst single accident on the south side of the mountain and one of the most devastating incidents ever to hit the Sherpa community. (An avalanche in 1922 on the north side of the peak took the lives of seven Sherpas.) In extreme environments, even when things feel relatively calm, there is still a significant amount of risk, as landscapes can change in an instant.

The Khumbu Icefall lies between base camp and Camp 1 on the Nepal side of Mount Everest, and it is one of the deadliest parts of the mountain. This section of the route rises 2,000 feet and looks like an obstacle course from some wild science fiction movie. The entire thing is comprised of massive ice towers called seracs, which can be as large as school buses. Or houses. The Icefall, which is part of an enormous glacier, is always in a state of motion, and it moves at a rate of about four feet per day. When the sun comes out and the ice softens, these building-size ice chunks start to shift around. Every once in a while, one or more of them will collapse onto the route, so climbers are in constant danger of being crushed. Picture yourself trying to make your way through a gigantic life-size game of Jenga, but instead of wood the blocks are made of ice. When the wrong piece moves, the entire structure can come crashing down, demolishing everything around it.

To increase the chance of making it through without incident, climbers typically start their journey through the Icefall in the early morning hours. It's not unusual to begin at 3:00 a.m. so that you finish the trip (or at least get through most of it) when things are still fairly frozen. Once day breaks and things begin to warm up, the Icefall becomes more unstable and potentially more dangerous.

Maneuvering through this area is made even more complicated by the fact that there are huge crevasses everywhere that add yet another layer of serious danger. At the onset of each climbing season, the Sherpas who are working as the Icefall Doctors prepare the Icefall for climbers by spanning rickety aluminum ladders over the largest of the various crevasses so that the climbers can cross from one side to the other without plunging to their deaths. Some sections of the Icefall require two, three, or even more ladders to be strung together in order for climbers to pass over crevasses or up steep walls of ice.

When you try to walk or crawl across multiple ladders that have been strung together, they bounce, they sway, they creak, and they can *really* freak you out. Keep in mind that you are maneuvering across these ladders at an elevation of more than 18,000 or 19,000 feet, so it's tricky to balance— especially if your feet are too small to span two ladder rungs. So when you're trying to make your way across a gargantuan crevasse and you're perched up on a ladder and it starts to sway or dip, it can be really scary (like, "Clean up on aisle four" kind of scary).

To increase safety, fixed lines of rope are laced throughout the Icefall so that climbers can clip into the lines and perhaps be spared a fall if the ladders should happen to give way or, say, the ground supporting the ladders should unexpectedly open up. While the avalanches and falling seracs remain constant threats that cannot be prevented, clipping into the fixed safety lines can indeed lessen the risk somewhat for climbers when it comes to crevasse falls or losing balance on a ladder.

When my teammates and I were making our final pass through the Icefall in 2002, heading down to base camp for the last time, a large chunk of the Icefall collapsed right behind us, leaving a climber dangling from a ladder by one wrist. Because he was able to move quickly and had properly clipped himself to a safety line, he survived the death trap and walked away from that jungle of ice, shaken but relatively unharmed. It was one of the most dramatic things I have ever witnessed. He was one of the lucky ones. Similar accidents have claimed many lives over the years.

The Icefall's fearsome and well-deserved reputation sometimes plays a role in people's decision to climb Everest from the north side, approaching from Tibet. Even the Sherpas who make the mountain home for several months each season (and are generally more comfortable on its slopes than many of the foreign climbers) fear the Icefall. When they stock camps higher up the mountain, they carry the heaviest loads they can possibly manage to minimize the number of times they must travel through the Icefall. It's pretty standard for the Sherpas to blow past the rest of us when going through the Icefall, since they are more practiced. The Sherpas gracefully dance across the ladders and make it look effortless, while the rest of us cautiously balance our way across, hoping like hell we don't fall into the abyss below. Here's the thing, though: Sherpas and other climbers who feel pretty confident on this tricky terrain don't always take the proper precautions to ensure their safety. Often their sense of security is false.

One of the first of many casualties of the 2012 climbing season was Namgyal Tshering Sherpa, who fell into a crevasse in the Khumbu Icefall and died. This was such a heartbreaker because had he clipped into the fixed lines, he probably would have survived the fall. Namgyal was an experienced climber and had summited Everest twice—in 2010 and 2011. He might have made it a third time had he simply followed the proper safety protocol.

It's easy to become complacent when something seems routine. Flying though the Icefall with the greatest of ease is commonplace for the Sherpas, so some of them skip the essential step of clipping into the ropes—which takes only a few seconds to do. If someone has failed to take the proper precautions and has gotten away with it fifty times, they don't think to do anything differently. But once in a while, on the fifty-first time, it doesn't work out.

Continuing risky behavior because you've gotten away with it in the past is a serious form of complacency, and it also sets a dangerous example for others. On one of my trips through the Icefall, a young guy climbing just ahead of me often failed to clip into the safety lines. Maybe he observed some Sherpas not following safe climbing protocol, and for some reason he thought it was okay for him to do the same. His skills were nowhere near the skills of the Sherpas, but he was too naïve to realize that. The guides noticed his behavior and suggested that he clip into the ropes, but he didn't seem to listen. When we were about two-thirds of the way though the Icefall he turned around and asked those of us behind him, "Does it bother you that I don't clip into the ropes?"

He apparently thought he was so skilled that he didn't need to worry about safety. I answered, "No, no, not at all."

Why would it bother me? Hell, I wasn't going to be responsible for the costs associated with repatriating his body. His rich parents would be writing that check. Okay, I'm being sarcastic here; I definitely didn't want to see anything bad happen to this guy. But by putting himself in danger, he was increasing the chances of an accident that would require other climbers to spend time on dangerous terrain trying to rescue him (or recover his corpse). Later on, another climber also failed to clip into the fixed ropes in the Icefall, and she sustained severe injuries to her face and spine in a fall. Only then did this careless young man modify his behavior.

Unfortunately, not all accidents in the Icefall are avoidable. The six Sherpas who perished in the 1970 avalanche were just in the wrong place at the wrong time. The mountain is a dangerous place and that's not going to change, which makes it all the more important to find ways to increase your odds of survival.

But if you can't make the ground more stable or prevent a serac from falling, how do you mitigate your risk, given you have to travel through this area multiple times throughout your two-month expedition? How do you stack the deck in your favor when you are dealing with a landscape that is constantly changing and impossible to predict? Is there anything you can do to increase the odds of emerging on the other side not only unscathed, but also in a position of strength? Yes. And the key is *agility*. You move swiftly, you move efficiently, and you remain ready to act and to react quickly as the environment around you is shifting and changing. While you won't eliminate the risk, you'll significantly reduce it and therefore increase your chances of survival.

The Khumbu Icefall taught me one of the most critical lessons about mountaineering, business, leadership, and life: fear is fine, but *complacency will kill you.*

Don't ever beat yourself up for feeling scared or intimidated. Fear is a natural human emotion, and it's a strong survival instinct that keeps us alert and aware of our surroundings. But fear doesn't have to keep us from pursuing a challenge. The real danger often comes from failing to react to shifts in the world around us—whether those changes take the form of a collapsed ladder, a sudden avalanche, regulatory changes within an industry, changes in consumer behavior, competitive threats, or the evolution of our chosen professional fields. In our work as well as when climbing, complacency can lead to extinction, threatening our livelihoods and our lives.

With all the unpredictable, uncontrollable shifts that occur in the mountains or in life, it's important to be prepared to deal with change. In the Icefall, climbers never know how or when the landscape will change, but they know damn well that the monstrous blocks of ice surrounding them are going to keep moving, so if they are going to survive, they have to keep moving, too. This isn't an area where you can hang out and take rest breaks. It's not the place to stop and call your mom on your satellite phone and wish her happy Mother's Day (believe me, she won't be happy to hear that you're calling her from the shade of a sixty-foot serac). The key to increasing your chance of survival is to get through the area as fast as you can while keeping your eyes and ears open for sudden shifts in the ice. Because the environment is constantly changing shape, you may need to reroute yourself on occasion if a section that was safe to cross the last time no longer looks safe. You expect the landscape to constantly evolve, and while you don't know exactly what it will look like from one hour to the next, you remain in a state of readiness to react to whatever changes come about.

The bottom line here is that agility is key to survival. To increase your speed through the Icefall, you need to increase your proficiency in ladder crossings, rappelling steep faces, and climbing vertical pitches. If you're skilled in these things, you will move through the Icefall faster. Of course, proficiency between 18,000 and 20,000 feet is different from proficiency at sea level, so you want to practice these skills at altitude.

The following is an excerpt from my 2010 expedition journal:

April 18. Yesterday was our first foray into the dreaded Khumbu Icefall, which is 2,000 vertical feet of massive ice chunks that are unstable and can topple over at any time. The terrain is nonstop unevenness, and just about every step you take has to be carefully positioned. Crevasses are everywhere, and the ones that are too big to jump over have aluminum ladders across them to help us get to the other side. Everyone did pretty well navigating the terrain. We were really prepared, and that's because ever since we arrived at base camp we have spent every day practicing our ice-climbing and ladder-crossing skills. Being in good climbing shape is only one small part of the equation for success on a big mountain like this—technical expertise is also important.

Because the Icefall is constantly changing shape, you can't always count on ladders being where you want them to be. For example, there could be a 30' vertical wall of ice that has a ladder going up it one day, and as the Icefall melts that ladder could fall into a crevasse the next day, so you have to find a way to get up and down that pitch minus the assistance from any Home Depot accessories. So, in order to prepare for this type of situation, we practiced on a 25' ice wall just outside of base camp and everyone took turns going up and down it with just two standard ice axes (vs. proper ice-climbing tools, which we do not have with us, but improvisation is always going to come into play in the mountains). It was challenging, to say the least, given we are at about 17,600' of elevation here at base camp.

Actually, *every* activity seems challenging at 17,600', and I get winded just walking from my tent to the mess tent for meals. (Much to my disappointment, there is no room service here. I must have misread the brochure.) We spent hours practicing our Icefall skills—ascending the ice wall and rappelling down the backside—and also practiced going across/up/down aluminum ladders in crampons. At one point my teammate Greg was descending the ice wall and somehow managed to... um...well, let's just say the family jewels may have lost some of their value. How much, I'm not sure exactly. All I know is that I was standing on the other side of the ice wall practicing my rappelling techniques, and I heard him screaming out in pain (and it sounded unusually high-pitched)—must have been a problem with the way his carabiner was positioned on the front of his harness, not sure, really—didn't want to ask as I figured it was a *sore* subject. He came down from the ice wall and was doubled over in pain. He's a pretty tough guy, though, so I'm sure he'll recover.

*Anyway...*the ice wall was not our favorite thing to practice on—just hard to do without the right tools and at 17,600' of elevation, but we all knew we needed to do it in order to be able to travel quickly through the Icefall as a team. After all nine of us went up and down the ice wall once, it was time to cycle through a second time. I was dreading doing it again, because I was pretty winded after several hours of ice climbing and rappelling and ladder practice. One by one, seven of my climbing partners went up and down that ice wall a second time, and it was now down to Greg and me to finish up the rotation. Vern Tejas, one of the most senior guides on the mountain, looked at Greg and said, "Your turn to go up again, Greg." Greg replied, "No can do. My balls hurt." He had a pretty legit excuse for not getting up on the ice wall obstacle course again. Since Greg was out, I knew it was my turn next, but I was so comfortable sitting on a rock nursing my bruised knees from some of the previous exercises, and I didn't want to move. Vern looked over at me and called for me to come over and give the ice wall another shot, but before he could get the last syllable of my name out of his mouth I looked up and quipped, "Uh, my balls hurt, too!!!!!" thinking I might be able to weasel my way out of having to climb again.

But he didn't buy it for some reason (maybe I don't have a good poker face, I don't know) and rolled his eyes and laughed and motioned for me to get myself up that ice wall again. I huffed and puffed as I struggled up the frozen wall with an ice axe in each hand, strategically placing the pick of each axe so that it would hold me as I struggled to find a good foothold....I jammed the front points of my crampons straight into the ice and moved my way up, and eventually I made it up and back down in one piece. It wasn't the climbing itself that was hard—I've done plenty of ice climbing in the past, just not at 17,600 feet, and *everything* seems like a huge effort at this elevation, as we are not yet properly acclimatized. And of course we never like to practice the skills we are weak in, because it is always more fun to perform the things we are good at—especially when there is an audience there. Practicing on the ice wall near base camp wasn't just about building confidence—it was about getting in the groove of moving quickly, because speed matters in that icefall. The faster you can get through it, the less time you spend in it, and the lower your chances are of dying before you reach the next camp.

Because the Icefall is by far the most unpredictable part of the route on Everest, climbers tend to have their guard up when making their way through it. But risk is everywhere on big mountains, and the risk exists *all the time*, even when things feel calm. Some of the world's most talented climbers have lost their lives because they let down their guard—they got a little complacent—when things seemed to be under control. Accidents like this feel even more devastating than when loss of life results from some extreme force of nature.

———————

Babu Chiri Sherpa started climbing as a teenager. He never attended school but taught himself to read. By age thirty-five he had reached Everest's summit ten times (one shy of the record at the time), climbing from both the north and the south sides of the mountain. He also held two world records; in 1999 he set the record for the most time spent on the summit (he was there for more than 21 hours without supplemental oxygen), and in 2000 he set the speed record for the fastest ascent (16 hours, 56 minutes). He was known all over the world and was one of the few Sherpas sponsored by an American company (Mountain Hardwear). Many of those familiar with Babu's accomplishments considered him one of the greatest climbers of all time.

Babu died on April 29, 2001, when he fell into a crevasse at Camp 2 while out walking around taking pictures. He was outside alone, so no one realized he was missing. His body was found the next day. It was a heartbreaking end to the life of perhaps the most celebrated Sherpa of his time. What made the accident exceptionally tragic was that it didn't happen on a knife-edge ridge or a steep ice face or in the Khumbu Icefall. Babu was just walking around Camp 2 (Advanced Base Camp), a relatively comfortable and safe camp (compared to the camps higher up on the mountain). Everyone walks around ABC freely without much fear of, well, anything. Babu's death rocked not only the Sherpa community but the entire climbing community. Typically bodies are not brought down from the mountain, but because Babu was one of the most accomplished and well-loved Sherpas, his body was recovered and he was given a proper burial. Babu, who had six daughters, was a huge proponent of education and dreamed of building a school in the village where he lived. That dream was realized after his death when a school was built in his honor. More than ten years after his death, he still remains an inspiration.

Avoiding complacency isn't just about keeping yourself in check; it also means watching out for all of your teammates. It's tempting to want to get in the zone when you climb. You have to work at finding your rhythm and timing your breaths with your steps so that you can keep a steady pace without having to stop and gasp for air. Your mind tends to wander when you're struggling up or down the slopes of a mountain for eight, ten, or twelve hours at a time. But as a leader it's important to stay engaged and to pay attention to the people around you, observing their behavior and taking action to keep them safe. And since everyone is in a leadership position on a climb, it's always going to be your job to check out your climbing partners and to make sure their gear is all set and all of their equipment is in working order. Even something as simple as losing a crampon can kill a climber if it happens on a steep slope. Likewise, a harness that's not properly buckled can come right off a climber; when that happens on high-angle terrain, it's all over.

Marty Hoey, one of the top female climbers in the world, fell to her death during an attempt to scale Everest via a new route on the peak's north side in 1982. She was thirty-one years old and aiming to be the first American woman to summit Everest. Marty had been a guide for thirteen years, had climbed Mount Rainier more than a hundred times, and had extensive experience on big peaks, with successful climbs of Peak Lenin (23,406 feet) in the former Soviet Union and

Nanda Devi (25,634 feet) in India. After her death her climbing partners concluded that she had not fastened her harness buckle correctly, as the harness was still attached to the rope when she fell 6,000 feet down the Great Couloir on the north side of Everest. The climbers were at 26,600 feet of elevation at the time, where the frigid temperatures make dexterity a challenge and the lack of oxygen makes it hard to think clearly. Having been up that high, I can personally attest to the fact that it is very easy to think to yourself, *Oh, my harness will hold just fine. The waist belt isn't going anywhere.* Marty's team did end up making an attempt to reach the summit, but between the bad weather and their heavy hearts, the team just did not have it in them to continue to press on. Lou Whittaker, the expedition leader, said that Marty's accident "dealt a mortal blow to our motivation. Our spirit was gone."

Marty's accident occurred because she had failed to rethread the end of the waist belt back through the harness buckle (known as "double-backing"). The tragedy is that this fatal error was so avoidable. Marty was an incredibly accomplished and well-respected climber, and her passing left the climbing community in a state of emotional shock. I have to believe that she is up there somewhere smiling at the number of women in the mountains these days, many of whom she inspired. I was not lucky enough to know Marty, but every time I do a harness check—on myself or on a teammate—I think of her.

Another tragedy, just as sad, just as avoidable: Todd Skinner, one of the world's best rock climbers, died while descending a route on Leaning Tower in Yosemite National Park in California in 2006. He was forty-seven years old with a wife and three kids. He had made dozens of first ascents on some of the world's most challenging routes. Skinner was

a pioneer of "free climbing," which is a form of rock climbing where ropes and protective hardware are used only to
prevent a fall. By contrast, many climbers on difficult routes
use rope or other gear as a means of moving higher on the
route. But free climbers would not use any equipment to
help them get past a tricky section of a rock climb.

Skinner was a legend, having completed the first free
ascents of the Salathe Wall on El Capitan in Yosemite and
the East Face of Trango Tower in Pakistan. He was incredibly charismatic and was in heavy demand as a motivational
speaker to corporate audiences. Skinner died when the
belay loop on his harness broke. A belay loop is a piece of
webbing that connects the waist belt to the leg loops, and it
is also where the carabiner is attached for belaying or rappelling. At some point prior to that climbing trip, Skinner
had realized his belay loop was worn and had ordered a
new harness, but it had not yet arrived. So he continued to
climb using the old harness.

Experienced climbers know to retire a harness as soon as
it shows signs of wear. Skinner knew the loop was worn yet
continued to climb with it. Harnesses are neither expensive
nor difficult to find. They're easy to replace. But it's also easy
to say, "Oh, it'll be fine for *one more climb*." Sadly, Todd didn't
get one more climb. These things happen. They will continue
to happen because we're all human. But you want them to
happen less often. So you look out for yourself. You look out
for each other. You check each other's crampons and you
check each other's harnesses. And then you check again.

Following the status quo is another mistake that people
and businesses often fall prey to. Sometimes the masses will
be zigging when the prudent thing to do is zag. And there
will often be times when those around you are moving

forward, but in fact the best decision for you is to stop. Different situations call for different types of actions, and as a leader it's up to you to evaluate all the circumstances before you in order to know what your best move is. It seems obvious, I know, but many leaders fail to do it; they just follow the crowd, assuming that everyone else is doing the right thing.

The spring of 2012 marked a more difficult season on Everest than usual for a number of reasons: It was a low snow year, so the route through the Icefall was less stable than in typical seasons. The temperatures were also warmer than normal, so even at the coldest hours of 2:00 or 3:00 a.m. the Icefall represented increased danger. Debris falling from the West Ridge added yet more hazards. An avalanche that came down from Nuptse (a 25,790-foot neighboring mountain) spilled over onto Everest and hit Camp 1. The incident caused injuries, but luckily there were no fatalities. The route up the Lhotse Face, which connects Camp 2 with Camp 3, was also less stable than usual, with significant (and potentially lethal) rockfall coming from higher up on the mountain. It's bad enough worrying that someone's water bottle will career down the Lhotse Face and kill or critically injure you, but adding to that the higher-than-usual rockfall danger makes that stretch of the route even more treacherous. Things got so bad on the Lhotse Face that sections of the route had to be shifted midseason to reduce the risk to the climbers.

Good leadership can also mean retreating when necessary. Russell Brice, one of the most well-known and experienced expedition leaders on Everest, made one of the boldest and controversial decisions during the 2012 spring climbing season when he called off his expedition five weeks into the trip. That decision meant that no one on his team got a shot at the summit. On the Himex website, Brice summed up his decision to pull the plug on his expedition: "The danger [on the peak this season] is certainly past my parameters."

Imagine putting months, perhaps years, into training for an Everest expedition—and then all of a sudden it is game over because some guy makes a decision on your behalf. Think about what goes into making an Everest climb a reality: taking out a loan, perhaps mortgaging your house, raising the sponsorship money (or writing a check for the cost of the trip if you are able), buying or borrowing all of the required gear, getting the time off from work (with no pay), spending five weeks busting your butt on the mountain... and then *not* getting your shot at the top—and not because you weren't strong enough or because you got a respiratory infection or a gastrointestinal infection or because your equipment malfunctioned or because you got hypothermia or frostbite or you sprained your ankle or you broke your ribs or fractured your wrist when you fell off a ladder or because the weather was bad and who the hell expected a storm so early in the day when the weather reports looked clear or because your great-aunt Gladys died and you had to leave the trip early to go to her funeral in Des Moines—*but because your expedition leader pulled the plug on your trip.* Total bullsh*t, right? *Wrong.*

As a leader, Brice's job is to keep his climbing team and his Sherpas safe and out of harm's way. That is priority numero uno. Because Brice did not feel the conditions in the Icefall and on the Lhotse Face were conducive to (reasonably) safe climbing, he told everyone the expedition was ending early and they were to pack up and head home.

No one got refunds; the money they paid had already been spent on permits, Sherpa salaries, equipment, food, oxygen, and so on, but he did promise them a discount if they wanted to come back and try again another year.

The level of disappointment among the climbers on Brice's expedition had to be painfully high, but I think he did the right thing. Brice himself would not have climbed Everest in those conditions, and therefore he was not comfortable sending his team up the mountain. I admire him for making such a tough call knowing it could very well affect future business, since climbers might have been hesitant to sign on to one of his upcoming trips. Brice made a decision that he knew could hurt him financially, but he was acting in what he believed was in the best interests of his climbing team and his Sherpas.

That's what good leaders do—they *always* look out for their people first. The easy thing to do would have been for him to just let the expedition proceed as planned. But he was the expedition leader; people were relying on him (and paying him) to make good decisions, and he made the best one he could based on the information he had at the time. And while the climbers might not have been happy with his decision, they respected him for doing what he thought was best for his team. It took some brass, for sure.

Would it have been the right call for every expedition? Certainly not. These types of decisions all come down to an individual leader's level of risk tolerance, which varies from person to person. Leaders should never expect the people on their teams to take any risks that they would not be willing to take themselves. Brice's decision to leave the mountain was the right decision for him. The other leaders who chose to stay made the right decisions as well.

The year 2012 turned out to be a particularly deadly one on Everest, with ten fatalities. In addition to the poor route conditions, another contributing factor was that the predicted window of good weather that climbers look for in order to judge when it is "safest" to go for the summit was forecasted to arrive later in the season than normal. This resulted in large numbers of people going for the top on the few decent weather days, and the bottlenecks on the way to the summit caused issues.

The *CBS Evening News* did a story (as did every media outlet, it seemed) on the fatalities that season, and a reporter from the show interviewed me about what went wrong on the mountain. Most of the footage from my interview ended up on the cutting room floor, so when the segment aired it didn't reflect my views on the issues of the 2012 climbing season. I believe the media got it wrong, focusing almost entirely on the "overcrowding" on the mountain with little or no mention of the other issues that contributed to the higher-than-normal death rate.

The problems that occurred in 2012 didn't come about because Everest was a lot more crowded than usual. The issue was that there were fewer days where the weather was cooperative, so everyone wanted to take a shot at the top during those few precious days. Had there been more days of predicted good weather, the stories of the 2012 season would have been different. There have definitely been seasons on Everest with more fatalities, but 2012 garnered quite a bit of media attention due to social media and the advanced communication systems now available, which can bring blogs, photos, and videos right from the mountain into your living room in real time.

There was a lot of debate about what went wrong on

Everest in 2012. Was it the crowds? The narrow weather window? Global warming's impact on the terrain? Everyone in the climbing community, armchair mountaineers, and the media seemed to have different opinions about what caused the deaths and injuries on Everest. Regardless, Russell Brice's decision stands out as a gutsy and wise call, made for the right reasons: keeping his people—the Sherpas that he employed as well as the climbers who were with him that season—as safe as possible.

Complacency comes in many forms: doing something because everyone around you is doing it, or going through the motions out of habit. It can be characterized by not preparing, not making a move, not moving fast enough, or not being agile enough. Ironically, complacency is a risk that skyrockets when things are going well—when you feel *safe enough*. But it's not just adventurers in extreme environments who have to watch out for complacency—businesses can also do themselves in if they aren't able to adjust to the shifts in their environment. For example, take a look at Ford.

Ford was a company that at one point suffered from damaging complacency but was able to turn things around and come back from the brink. In the mid- to late 1990s the stock market was raging and fuel prices were low. Ford was flying high. They had acquired luxury brands Jaguar and Aston Martin and offered a diverse range of cars that would appeal to just about any demographic. But once the twenty-first century rolled in, things started to slide due to rising fuel prices, an unstable economy, and the high cost of legacy health care. But Ford continued to operate as it had in the previous decade, and as a result they did themselves a lot of damage.

When Allan Mulally left Boeing and took the helm of Ford in September 2006, the automaker barely had a pulse and was heading for a $17 billion loss in profits. Mulally knew he had to make some big moves in order to keep the company alive. He closed manufacturing plants, chopped thousands of jobs (ouch), and dumped Ford's luxury brands—adios, Jaguar, Land Rover, and Aston Martin (although Ford retained a small percentage of ownership in Aston Martin). Layoffs and the discontinuation of high-end brands don't exactly scream "growth," but the car industry was shifting, and Ford had to shift, too.

Mulally's decision to take the company in that direction was a sign that he knew they had to move quickly to eventually emerge as a better, stronger, and more agile company. He had to get rid of the corporate complacency. It worked. By 2009 the company was profitable again. The ascent continued: in 2011 Ford's net income was more than $20 billion, and more than 41,000 hourly wage workers received an extra $6,200 each through the profit-sharing plan. In July 2012 Ford announced they would be creating 12,000 new jobs. The company believes that by 2015, they will be producing 8 million vehicles a year (up from 5.53 million in 2008).

No discussion of complacency in the business world would be complete without a mention of Research in Motion (RIM), maker of the BlackBerry smartphone. RIM was founded in 1984, and its technology put mobile e-mail on the map. By 2008 the company was valued at more than $80 billion. By 2012 it was valued at less than $5 billion. RIM failed to adapt to the changing smartphone market. They didn't anticipate the wide acceptance of touchscreens, and even as these touchscreens gained in popularity by leaps and bounds, RIM still dismissed the demand for the technology. They kept thinking that the advantages of their physical keyboard (called a QWERTY keyboard) would keep customers coming back. It didn't. Web browsing and downloadable apps—who needs that? Um, *everyone*.

At one point RIM controlled approximately 50 percent of the smartphone market. But into their third decade, their market share was hovering somewhere between 2 and 7 percent. They failed to adapt to the shifting landscape in their industry. RIM came out with a new device in 2013, and as of this writing the jury is still out on whether they will make a comeback. (I'm rooting for them, as I am a QWERTY keyboard fan.) But they're learning the hard way that it's a lot more difficult to regain market share than to keep it in the first place. They'll have to find some serious momentum, because Apple and Google, two companies very adept at innovating, will continue to advance their products and platforms, so as soon as RIM launches the next-generation BlackBerry, they better be ready to look at what they need to do next to stay competitive in a fast-moving, ever-changing industry. Perhaps their board of directors needs a trip through the Khumbu Icefall to remind them of the dangers of complacency.

File under "Avoiding Complacency"

You must be able to act and react quickly to stay alive when you're in an environment that is constantly shifting. Don't ever take things for granted and assume that your position is safe. Even if the ground feels solid, it doesn't mean you can relax, because as soon as you are comfortable, everything will shift again. Look out for your teammates and help them avoid dangerous habits. Always be planning your next move, because *complacency can kill you.*

Chapter 6

COMING UP SHORT

Making the Most of Weakness

In extreme situations—when the stakes are exceptionally high, when the environment is precarious, and when the hurdles are extraordinarily tough—the way you deal with the weak link on your team often means the difference between success and failure.

In business, you will sometimes have to work with people who aren't nearly as good as you are—those who can't perform as well or match your skills. Weak colleagues are not hard to identify. I don't want to be cruel here, but let's face it: there's always that *one person* who seems to show up on every team—you know, the person everyone else secretly wishes would quit, transfer to another division, or get trapped under something heavy. These people, to put it bluntly, are liabilities in terms of the job you are trying to do. They lag behind, drag everybody else down, and hinder progress. If only they could perform at a higher level, or be smarter, or work more efficiently—or, even better, *just go away*—the entire team would be so much more productive. And happier!

And although it may be painful to even imagine this, there could even be a time when, in fact, *you* might be the one who can't cut it—when *you* are the person everyone else wishes would just go away, even if you are trying your hardest.

Most people confronted with a weakness in a team member or in themselves will insist on trying to overcome it. But that's a flawed approach, at least when it comes to improving human performance. Why? Because the harsh reality is this: there's a fairly strong chance that a weakness can *never* be overcome. I'm not talking about attitude, which is something people generally *can* change. I'm talking about physical limitations like height or speed, and mental skills like mathematical ability or the way our brains process information. There are aspects about each of us that are almost impossible to improve upon, and that won't change no matter how many self-help books we read or how many self-help gurus we see.

Yes, it's true that some of our abilities will improve with work experience, mentoring, and training, but the dirty little secret we are scared to admit—especially to ourselves or to an employer—is that there are a handful of things at which we will always suck.

But there is hope. You can excel despite your limitations, because even if you cannot *overcome* a weakness like height or size or lousy analytical or sales skills, you can always *compensate* for it. This is what you should focus on, especially as you face extreme challenges of any sort.

Compensating for a weakness is about leveraging hidden attributes in innovative ways that can move you, other people, and your whole team forward. Look at all of the incredibly successful entrepreneurs, executives, scientists, athletes, and artists who have learning or other types of disabilities. As kids, many of them got the message that they would never amount to anything because of their poor performance in school. John Chambers, diagnosed with dyslexia at age nine, went on to become the CEO of Cisco, a $40 billion networking company. Billionaire businessman Richard Branson also suffered from dyslexia, yet his tenacity, creativity, and ability to connect with others made up for his disability; he went on to found the travel, entertainment, and lifestyle conglomerate Virgin Group. Famed General Electric CEO Jack Welch never let his lifelong stammer get in the way of his career.

Leadership involves compensating for your own weakness and helping other people do the same for themselves. *Good leaders know it's their responsibility to help every team member become productive, so that everyone on the team benefits.* I experienced this firsthand during a historic trip across Antarctica a few years ago. I was part of a five-person international team of polar adventurers that set out to ski a six-hundred-mile remote route from the edge of the Ronne Ice Shelf in west Antarctica to the South Pole.

Obviously, the South Pole is a lot different from your typical work environment—even with your air-conditioning on full blast. But it's similar in that the workplace can be incredibly intense. Your job, your client, your promotion, your account, your reputation, your company's quarterly performance, and your employees' own well-being are on the line every single day. But you do not have to allow weakness, your own or someone else's, to add to the stress or threaten success. The events that unfolded for me in Antarctica provided real insight into how great leaders can effectively handle a weak link—and how the weak link can handle herself—in any environment.

The route that my team took in 2007–2008 is referred to as the Messner Route, because legendary Italian explorer Reinhold Messner was the first to complete it nearly twenty years earlier.

By the time we launched our expedition a couple of Norwegian teams had followed in Messner's tracks (um, no, not his actual ski tracks...), but no one from North America had ever made an attempt. The Messner Route is considered more challenging than the traditional route taken by most South Pole expeditions, because it has a significant amount of crevasse danger. Another thing that makes this kind of ski expedition challenging is that the surface of the ice is laden with sastrugi, which sounds a little like an Italian pastry (which would be awesome; there are no bakeries down there)—but they are actually ridges that have formed on the snow's surface from snow deposits and wind erosion, sort of like sand dunes but made of ice. Maneuvering over and around the sastrugi on skis can be quite dangerous.

The trip required more than just physical strength and an in-depth knowledge of crevasse-rescue techniques. The harsh Antarctic environment throws some serious psychological challenges at even the most experienced adventurers. First, there is very little visual stimulation. By that I mean there is essentially nothing to focus your eyes on. Out on the ice, the world appears white in every direction, with no surface features (other than the sastrugi) and no delineation between earth and sky. You look around and sometimes you really can't tell where the ground stops and the sky starts. This may sound like a kind of interesting novelty, and it is at first, but after a while it gets old—in a scarily disorienting way. And when I say this goes on all day, I mean *all day*, since you never really know when it's nighttime unless you look at your watch. The days mesh together thanks to twenty-four hours of sunlight, which makes sleeping another challenge. Then add the fact that Antarctica is the coldest, windiest place on earth, and it's clear you're definitely in one of the most extreme (and extremely bizarre) environments on the planet.

When I was researching the trip, I came across a paper published in 2007 in which Lawrence Palinkas, an anthropologist from the University of Southern California, defined a condition known as "polar madness." He described how people who spend extended periods of time in polar regions are at risk of, well, pretty much completely losing their minds because of the lack of visual stimulation combined with sleep deprivation and physical and mental exhaustion. Palinkas's paper cited examples of polar expeditions that ended in disaster, including a scientific mission in the 1880s that led to suicide and cannibalism. Only six of the twenty-five men in the group survived. (Note to self: *seek teammates who are vegetarians.*)

As for my polar jaunt, it pretty much looked like this: We were going to the coldest, windiest place on earth to attempt what is considered to be one of the harshest expeditions known to man. We would be covering six hundred miles of challenging terrain on skis while each hauling 150 pounds of our own gear and supplies in sleds that were harnessed to our waists. Our team of five would be pushing our bodies to their limits as our physical and mental conditions deteriorated over the course of the journey... and all the while we'd be hoping that that none of our teammates would develop polar madness and mistake an ice axe for one of those back scratchers that you get from the Sharper Image catalog.

An environment as extreme as Antarctica requires a unique set of skills because everyone's health and well-being are on the line, yet urgent medical care is not readily accessible. It can take days or even *weeks* to evacuate someone off the ice. That's why success isn't just about getting to the South Pole; it's about surviving the trip and coming back with all of one's fingers and toes intact. Not to mention one's mind.

Unfortunately, unlike each of my past corporate jobs, this gig didn't include a new-hire orientation to prepare me for my role on this team. I had no employee manual to walk me through the process. I was expected to show up, meet my teammates for the first time, and hit the cold Antarctic ground running (well, skiing). I was on my own to prepare.

I knew one of my greatest challenges would be my size. I was pretty sure I'd be much smaller than everyone else on the team, because I typically am. I am short and have a small frame, and there is no way around that. I'm not so short that I would ever have my own reality show, but short to the point where each of my teammates would probably have fifty to a hundred pounds on me. Size (and the sheer brute strength that goes along with it, which comes in handy when you're hauling a heavy sled across the ice) was definitely my biggest shortcoming (sorry), so I made sure I trained extra-hard during the three months that led up to the trip.

The best way to train for a polar expedition is to practice

what you'll be doing every day, which is skiing in subzero temperatures while dragging a mammoth sled across the ice. This is tough to set up in San Francisco. The next best thing is to simulate the activity. So I used a long rope to tie a car tire to a harness that I wore around my waist, and then I dragged the tire along the sand of a nearby beach to mimic the motion of dragging a heavy sled.

Several times a week for three months I trudged through the sand on Ocean Beach, dragging that tire behind me. Every step took an incredible amount of effort. I was struggling and grunting the entire time, but eventually I got used to dragging that tire, so I then added another one. Passersby definitely gave me some weird looks, most likely because the garbage that littered the beach would accumulate in the tires as I trudged across the coastline, so I amassed quite a collection of trash and debris. I must have looked like a homeless person who was using the tires to transport my earthly belongings. I say this because people kept coming up to me and offering me money.

Pulling those tires for miles and miles was hard. And it was also ridiculously boring—which was ideal training for the monotony I would face in Antarctica. I did get stronger, eventually working my way up to dragging three tires behind me. By the end of my training period, I had collected enough random remnants from the beach to make a lovely collage out of dead birds, beer bottles, syringes, and condom wrappers. I was ready to mount my own art show. I was also as ready as I could possibly be to hit the ice.

On November 27, 2007, the journey began. The expedition launched from Punta Arenas, Chile, the southernmost large city in the world. There, I met my four teammates. The team leader was Eric Philips, an Australian who has had more experience on the ice than Wayne Gretzky. We all hailed from different countries but had exchanged a few e-mails prior to the start of the trip, so we knew one another's names, but that was about it.

We spent the first three days sorting gear and organizing food supplies, which would account for the majority of the weight in our sleds. We needed to consume a minimum of 5,000 to 6,000 calories per day (based on the energy required to put in a full day of skiing while dragging a heavy sled in subzero temperatures). In order to meet our caloric intake goals we packed a lot of sticks of butter; butter is high in calories as well as fat, which we needed to keep us warm.

So how much butter did we bring? Glad you asked. Each of us packed an *entire stick of butter for every day of the trip.* Or at least that was what was recommended. I ended up packing less than that, because I was certain I couldn't down an entire stick every day. I could easily do it if I had a fresh sourdough baguette to go with it, but that wasn't happening. Eating plain butter is every bit as disgusting as it sounds, but you can't afford to run out of energy during a trip like this, so you choke it down. Otherwise, when you're too low on energy you risk hypothermia and frostbite. You burn hundreds of calories just trying to stay warm, so eating something every hour is pretty much mandatory.

A typical daily menu looks something like this: For breakfast, two packs of instant oatmeal with high-fat powdered milk, butter, and sugar. Lunch is comprised of instant noodles, a massive chocolate bar, chunks of salami, pieces of cheese, dried fruit, nuts, biscuits, a granola bar, and more butter (which you just try to get down any way you can— usually straight into your mouth with a spoon). A typical dinner would be freeze-dried meals supplemented with (surprise!) butter. Dessert? More chocolate, sugar, and butter. Then there were the between-meal snacks, which were bits of food from your lunch bag. Despite the huge amount of food we were consuming, each of us would come back from this trip having lost a significant amount of weight. *Don't hate us, Oprah!*

On December 4, after a day of weather delays, we took off on an Ilyushin 76, a plane designed in the Soviet Union for military use. About the size of a Boeing 767, it has four engines and can carry 88,000 pounds more than three thousand miles in less than six hours. The Ilyushin earns bragging rights for its ability to take off and land on short, crude runways. It's an ideal plane for this kind of trip, since the natural blue-ice runways in Antarctica make landings tricky.

Once we reached Antarctica, we boarded a smaller, ski-equipped Twin Otter plane for a one-and-a-half-hour flight to the Ronne Ice Shelf. The Ronne Ice Shelf is the western part of the Filchner-Ronne Ice Shelf, the second largest ice shelf in the world, spanning an area of 163,000 square miles just east of the Antarctic Peninsula. When the Twin Otter landed, we hopped out, unloaded all of our gear, and then watched as the plane flew out of sight, leaving us to fend for ourselves for the better part of the next two months. No turning back now. We decided to set up our tents and get a good night's sleep, knowing that the next six weeks would take a lot out of us.

We dubbed ourselves Team CAN DU—a play on the first letters that represented our citizenship: George Szwender was **C**anadian, Eric Philips was **A**ustralian, Merete Spilling Gjertsen was **N**orwegian, Bernice Notenboom was **D**utch, and of course I was a citizen of the **U**SA. This was George's idea, and I liked it. We all did. The name CAN DU evoked feelings of empowerment and determination. (We initially wanted to come up with a team name that would honor Reinhold Messner, since he'd pioneered our route, but the only idea we could come up with was "**S**outh **P**ole **E**xpedition **R**oute de **M**essner," which made for a rather unfortunate acronym.)

The next morning it was showtime. We strapped on our skis, kitted up, harnessed our sleds to our waists, and started on our journey. We covered more than twelve miles the first day, so we were really pleased we had such a strong start. But I was feeling it—even after day one. Every muscle in my body ached, especially my upper back and hip flexors. The way my body felt, the thirteen miles we covered on day two might as well have been thirteen hundred miles.

Dragging my sled across the snow and ice every day, and maneuvering around the sastrugi, was tougher than I'd imagined, thanks in part to the knee-deep snow. Our sleds were made of fiberglass with a gel-coat finish, and they felt even heavier in high snow. A sled that weighs more than the person pulling it wins the power struggle every time, and mine had a mind of its own. It was not always interested in following my ski tracks, and I took a few good falls that first week, bruising my wrist on day four, bruising my kneecaps on day five, and twisting my ankle on day six. Day seven was an injury-free day (hallelujah). I had a few blisters on my right foot, but my red toenail polish held up brilliantly, so I had that going for me, which was nice.

I was definitely feeling pretty banged up, but nothing that a few over-the-counter painkillers couldn't mask. But I kept my pains to myself, because no one wants to hear complaints when everyone is putting in eighty-hour workweeks, and I was sure other people were hurting, too. When there is a job to do and the team is counting on every member to pull his or her weight (in my case, this was literally true, and then some...), pushing through exhaustion and discomfort is the only feasible option.

We had to do our best to stick to a daily routine in order to make it to the South Pole without running out of food and supplies. Wake up at 6:00 a.m. Fire up the stoves to melt ice so we could fill water bottles and eat breakfast. Take down the tents, pack our sleds, and hit the ice by 8:30 a.m. We skied for nine hours each day with four short food and water breaks. We usually stopped skiing around 5:30 p.m., because at the end of each day we needed time and energy to set up camp and get settled in for the night. There's still plenty of work to do once you're done skiing.

Setting up tents was no small task, because each tent had to be protected from the elements. So after a full day of skiing we spent an hour digging up snow and forming ice bricks with a snow shovel to put around the outside of the tents. This ensured the tents wouldn't be destroyed by the winds. If we lost one tent it wouldn't end the trip; we'd still have two left. But it would make the rest of the trip even more insanely uncomfortable. Once the tents were secured, it was back to melting ice for hot drinks and our freeze-dried meals. We aimed to be asleep by 10:00 p.m. each night.

After a few weeks of sticking to this routine, we realized we were not covering enough ground. At the rate we were going, we would not make it to the South Pole before running out of food and supplies, so we had to change the schedule a bit. We added an extra hour to the day—up at 5:00 a.m., and then hit the ice by 6:30 a.m.—which allowed us (or forced us) to spend two more hours skiing.

Day after day after day we endured temperatures that

reached fifty degrees below zero and crazy strong winds that knocked me off balance a few times. My hands got so stone-cold some days during our rest breaks that it took me roughly thirty minutes to warm them back up to the point where I could use them (thank goodness for disposable hand warmers). Again, I kept these woes to myself. On an expedition like this, the elements really take a toll on your body, and it's not just the cold. Antarctica has twenty-four hours of daylight during its summer (December through February), and the sun reflects off the snow, making UV exposure a constant concern. I wore goggles (they protect your skin better than glacier glasses, which just protect your eyes) and a neoprene ski mask every day to cover my face—and even then I still didn't leave my tent in the mornings without slathering on sunscreen with SPF 70.

A couple of members of my team did not cover their faces for the first week and developed chilblains, which are ulcers that develop on the skin as a result of exposure to the extreme cold. They looked like they had just finished an ultimate fighting match: red, swollen faces covered in blisters that oozed pus and blood. Sometimes they would wake up throughout the night in pain from the blisters. Even eating and drinking became a challenge, as touching anything to their lips caused them to wince in pain. So while my skin remained intact, it was, unfortunately, the only part of me that was holding up well.

Even though we each had our own aches and pains, I was by far the slowest and physically weakest member of our team. How could this be? I had trained my *ss off hauling tires along the beach for weeks. But you know what will always trump training? *The laws of physics.* No matter how hard I tried every day, I could not keep up with my teammates, who were bigger and taller and, hell, stronger than I was or ever will be. Even the next smallest person dwarfed me in size and had fifty pounds on me. George, our Canadian teammate, was six foot four and 230 pounds (a full foot taller and more than twice my weight), so basically the law of physics dictated that no matter how much I trained for this expedition, George was going to be able to haul that mother of a sled faster and more efficiently than I could. I was just too small and my short legs could not span the same distance versus my taller teammates. My Norwegian teammate, Merete, kept trying to make me feel better by telling me that she was only able to ski so quickly because she had been born with skis on her feet (damn those Norwegians!). I told her that for the sake of her mother, I hoped she had been delivered via C-section.

I felt so awful about my inability to keep up that I wished I could fall into a hole and die (but then I stopped wishing for that, because the chances of that happening were actually pretty decent given there was a significant amount of crevasse danger along our route).

Any of you type A overachievers wondering what it's like to be the slowest, weakest, most pathetic member of a team? All of you Harvard Business School grads who are shaking your heads "no," listen up: It feels absolutely horrible. Especially when there is no way to camouflage the fact that you are definitely the worst performer in the group. And it feels even more miserable when you know you are hurting the team's chances of success.

I was so self-conscious about my lack of speed that this occupied my every thought. I was sure that the rest of the team was unhappy with me because of my slower pace, but if they were, they certainly didn't show it. They were always patient; they'd stop for breaks and wait for me to catch up. But every time I saw them waiting up ahead for me, I would burn myself out trying to catch up as quickly as I could. And then by the time I skied up to them and caught my breath, it was time to take off again.

Falling a few minutes behind the group on a mountaineering expedition is not a huge deal, but it is a *very* big deal on a polar expedition, where it takes only a few minutes for people on skis to travel quite far. Under normal circumstances, waiting around for someone is simply an annoyance akin to holding the elevator door open for a straggling colleague when you're racing to get out of the office so you get to happy hour before the $6 pitchers of beer double in price. But in Antarctica, waiting around even for a few minutes is indeed a huge concern, because moving is really the only way to stay warm. If people have to stand around, they get *really* cold. But slowing the pace down significantly to accommodate my speed (or lack thereof) could have jeopardized our chances of getting to the South Pole before we ran out of food and supplies. We had to cover a certain number of miles every day in order to stay on schedule.

The thought of holding up my teammates caused me to double down on my own frustration. Every time I caught up to them I apologized profusely. "I am so sorry, so sorry, guys—keep going keep going, you really *don't* have to wait for me. I'm fine. Just go." They smiled and insisted it was no problem, but I figured they would tire of this drill fairly quickly. I also convinced myself that everyone on my team was wishing I were not a part of their expedition. I was beginning to wish the same thing, because the truth was that I would not get any better at dragging that sled. My body simply would not let me. But I also knew I wasn't going to quit, because my psyche would not let me—and because quitting is just not an option when you are in the middle of Antarctica. There's literally nowhere to go! It's not like you can head into the ski lodge and get a cup of hot cocoa or catch the shuttle bus back to the parking lot so you can get your car. I continued to struggle, day in and day out.

———

About five days into the trip, I was cooking my dinner in my tent, feeling pretty depressed about my inability to perform at the same level as my teammates. I secretly wished I would have a trip-ending injury that would alleviate them of the burden of having me as part of Team CAN DU. While we were still a long way from the South Pole, which is the actual bottom of the world, I felt like I had already reached my personal low point. Suddenly, I overheard Eric, our team leader, and George, the twice-my-size teammate, quietly talking in the nearby tent they shared. It was as if a coworker had accidentally butt-dialed me while he was talking to our boss. I was fairly sure I was about to hear them rip into my performance. I don't remember the exact conversation word for word, but I will never ever forget the gist:

"Alison is really struggling with the weight of her sled." To my relief, Eric genuinely seemed concerned.

Then George piped in. "Yeah, she is. I feel bad for her because she is trying *so hard* to keep up, but she's so much smaller than everyone else."

"We should try to help her out somehow. Maybe we could offload some of the weight in her sled."

"Great idea, Eric. Let's do it."

I was completely shocked by this conversation. I'd convinced myself that my teammates wanted to get rid of me because I was the weakest person on the team. But instead, these two men were secretly strategizing on how to *help* me. I was especially surprised at their proposed solution, because offloading weight from my sled onto other people's would make their loads even heavier—assuming they did not intend to toss my food supply and clothing into a crevasse.

The next morning, Eric and George emerged from their tent, stretched their arms, and exchanged the usual "good mornings" with the rest of us. Of course they had no idea that I had been privy to their conversation the previous night. Then they began their charade. "Hey, George, help me out with something," said Eric. "I want to make sure that everyone's sleds are about equal weight so I know that we're all hauling about the same amount of gear and supplies. Grab the end of that sled, will ya, mate?"

He nodded for George to help him, and the two of them began the process of picking up each team member's sled so that they could judge whether the group's gear had been evenly distributed based on how heavy each sled felt. I watched as George and Eric each grabbed an end of Merete's sled. "This one feels about right." They dropped it back down onto the ice. Then they grabbed Bernice's sled. "This one feels pretty good, too." They also picked up each of the sleds they had been hauling. "These feel like they are about what they should be," and they gently laid the sleds back down.

Then they walked to my sled. Each grabbed an end and began to lift it. After raising it just a few inches off the ground, their faces winced and contorted as if this effort of lifting were causing them excruciating pain. Almost on cue, they simultaneously dropped my sled like it was a grand piano. It hit the ice with a thud, and Eric clutched his back as if he had really hurt himself. "What the hell is in this sled?"

George continued the theatrics: "I don't know, but it's waaaay too heavy. What on earth is in here?"

Eric, still acting as if he had pulled something in his back or slipped a disc, looked over at me. "Ali, I don't know what you've got in your sled, but it's *much* heavier than the others. You're carrying more than anyone else on this team. This is crazy! You should let us take some weight out in order to make things a little more even. There's no reason why you should be carrying so much more than the rest of us."

I stood there, speechless. Sure, their acting was pretty bad, but I was beyond moved by what these men were trying to do. I had never witnessed such a display of teamwork during an expedition. Not only were they willing to carry some of my weight—which would in turn increase their own sleds' weight and make their work on the ice tougher—but the way they handled the situation blew me away. Consider the tack they could have taken:

"Hey, Alison, we're all getting tired of waiting for you, so we're going to lighten your load so that you can move faster even though it means more work for us." Publicly pointing out something that was already obvious to me and the team would have only made me feel worse, not to mention humiliated. Imagine how crappy you would feel if the head of HR posted your lame performance review on the front of the fridge in the break room. Even if Eric and George had approached me privately and said the same thing, I would have felt more self-conscious every minute of every day for the rest of the trip. George and Eric knew I already felt bad about my pace, and they understood that cratering my morale, versus boosting it, would not do anyone any favors in the middle of Antarctica. They demonstrated amazing leadership not only by helping me compensate for my weakness by reducing the weight of my sled, but also by *how they went about it.* By taking my emotional well-being into account, they made it clear that they cared about me as a teammate and wanted me to succeed. I'll never forget it.

I went along with their plot. I was beyond grateful to them for the way they handled the situation. They unloaded some of my food bags and fuel canisters and packed them into their own sleds. When we hit the ice again, not only was my sled less heavy but my heart was as well.

I immediately began to think of how I could return the favor—even though I was not supposed to know that they had done me a favor. I wanted to ensure that Eric and George never regretted their decision. I came up with a perfect idea: a way to use my height to help, not hinder.

As I described, one of the important but exhausting jobs that must get done every night is securing each tent by making ice blocks, or snow bricks, and then stacking them along the perimeter of each tent to protect the tent from potential damage caused by the elements. Shoveling snow and ice was the last thing anyone wanted to do at the end of a fifteen-hour day spent skiing, but it was an important part of our routine that could not be avoided.

I'd previously noticed that it was somewhat awkward for George to shovel snow because he was so tall. To effectively use the twenty-four-inch snow shovel required a lot of effort to make contact with the ground, and bending down over and over again was an uncomfortable endeavor. But because I was so short and closer to the ground, I could use the shovel more easily than the taller guys, since I didn't have to strain my back in order to bend over. A lightbulb went on in my head.

That evening, I grabbed a shovel and walked over to

George and Eric as they were pitching their tent. "Hey, guys, may I shovel the snow around your tent?" They looked at me like I was from another planet. "Yeah," I continued. "I really want to shovel the snow to hold down your tent."

George looked puzzled. "You do?" he asked.

"*Yes!*" I almost begged. "Because I love to shovel snow. Love it love it. *Love. It!* See," I went on, improvising, "I grew up in Phoenix. Yeah, in Phoenix. And, well, I never ever got to shovel snow growing up, so now I really love to do it and I rarely get an opportunity to shovel like this, so it's really a huge treat for me to be able to shovel snow and I try to do it as much as I can whenever I have the chance."

George looked at me as if I were losing my mind. *Polar madness*, he surely thought. So I just grabbed the shovel and got to work, silently, efficiently, as if it were part of my normal routine.

Every time I had an opportunity to shovel snow for Eric and George, I did. There was not one single minute during the entire rest of the trip that I was not aware that my teammates were pulling more than their fair share of weight in order to help me out. Me, the weak link, the smallest, slowest team member, the most worthless when it came to hauling weight. I was aware that my increased speed also helped the team, but because of Eric and George's commitment to my physical and emotional well-being, I was determined to find other ways to become an invaluable member of the team. I would never overcome the fact that I could not pull the same amount of weight as my larger teammates, but I felt I could—and should—contribute in other ways.

Leaders aren't the only people on a team responsible for strengthening the weak link. The team member with the problem must also take responsibility for his or her progress.

If that's you, face your shortcoming instead of whining about it, hiding it, blaming circumstances, or bitching about it to others. Accept that you might just really suck at certain things or at certain times. Once you acknowledge it, then look for unexpected, untraditional ways to effectively contribute. Sometimes only you know what your strengths are, so you must constantly and consciously think about areas where you can add value.

My solution was not rocket science. I simply observed my teammates and identified a way to assist them that played to my strengths. Being short offers more advantages than just airline seat comfort, and I made my size an asset in the circumstances.

———

On January 12, 2008, our team arrived at the lowest point on earth, the geographic South Pole. We spent two days camped outside the Amundsen-Scott South Pole Station and then bid good-bye to that big white monster of a continent and flew back to civilization. During our first real meal in nearly two months (where we ordered steak, red wine, and actually had bread with our butter) we celebrated our journey and reminisced about our favorite moments and most vivid memories of the experience. Eric mentioned that one of the things that he would never forget was how much I liked to shovel snow and added that he had never met anyone who enjoyed making snow barriers as much as I did.

At that point I had to confess. "I frickin' *hate* shoveling snow! Are you kidding me? The only reason I pretended to like shoveling snow was because you pretended that my sled weighed too much in order to have an excuse to take a bunch of weight out of it."

The look on Eric's face revealed that he was honestly surprised that I knew all about his and George's shenanigans. Apparently, I was a much better actor than either of them. I continued, "I overheard you guys talking in your tent, and I knew exactly what you were doing."

Eric laughed and smiled. "You heard that?"

I nodded and smiled back. What I heard that night was so much more than a plan being hatched. I heard what compassionate human beings sound like. I heard what a committed teammate sounds like. And I heard what a true leader sounds like.

File under "Handling the Weak Link"

Most people, no matter how talented, will at some point find themselves in a position where one or more of their skills don't measure up to the skills of those around them. Great leaders find unexpected ways to bring out the best in themselves and in others. Do whatever you have to do in order to make everyone on your team feel like they're valuable contributors. And instead of expecting others to overcome a weakness, get creative and find ways to help them *compensate*, which often involves leveraging hidden talents. Ultimately, you and your organization will be stronger for it.

Muhammad Ali, who struggled in school because he was learning disabled, was quoted as follows: "I never said I was the smartest, I said I was the greatest." It's your job to help people be the greatest.

Chapter 7

BRING IT

You Need Your A-Game, and Then Some

Leaders are supposed to know what skills and equipment are needed to get a job done right or to achieve a goal. If you have one but not the other—if you have the right skills but don't have the right equipment—you'll fail.

In June 1941, Germany invaded the Soviet Union with millions of armed soldiers and hundreds of thousands of tanks and horses—everything you need to wage a battle successfully. Um, *almost.* The Germans didn't bring warm clothes or tools to maintain their equipment through the Russian winters. Once the frigid weather set in, many German soldiers suffered from severe frostbite, and their tanks and other weapons couldn't function in the freezing temperatures. Historians have lots of theories about why the German attack on the Soviet Union failed, but most agree that one big problem was this: they didn't pack well.

Of course the Nazi state's blunder was a good thing for

humankind, but you get the point I'm trying to make. You can put plenty of financial resources and manpower behind an effort, but if you don't bring the proper gear, tools, or equipment, you'll have a tough time achieving your desired outcome.

One of the scariest experiences I have ever had in the mountains, one that nearly cost me my life, was a result of simply not having the proper equipment available when I needed it.

I blame my near-death experience on poor leadership. I had been climbing for just over a year when this incident occurred. I was a decent climber for someone who was new to the sport, but I still lacked some of the judgment that climbers gain only through experience. Looking back on it now, the climbing leader's mistakes seem blatantly obvious to me, but at the time I simply didn't know better. I had seen others make the same mistakes many times before and nothing bad ever happened to them. They got lucky. This time, however, luck was nowhere to be found.

It was October 1999. I had decided that my fall break from graduate school would be the ideal time to attempt to scale Carstensz Pyramid—a 16,024-foot towering limestone peak, the highest peak in Australasia, and thus one of the Seven Summits.* We were on six-week terms during the academic year, and I had a week off from classes in between

---

* There are two versions of the Seven Summits: One version includes Carstensz Pyramid, since it is the highest peak in Australasia (the region comprised of Australia, New Zealand, the island of New Guinea, and the neighboring islands in the Pacific Ocean). The alternative version includes the easier-to-climb Mount Kosciuszko (the highest peak in mainland Australia), which does not require any technical skills and is an easy hike to 7,310 feet/2,228 meters.

terms, so with the weekends on both ends that gave me nine full days—ten if I could fly out on the same day of my final exams at the end of the first term. The minimum length of time for a Carstensz expedition is ten days. That can work if everything goes as planned (which, of course, never happens).

It's standard practice to factor in several extra days for travel delays, health issues, extra acclimatization, bad weather...let's see...tribal warfare, ankle sprains, snake-bites.... Anyway, most climbers purchase open-ended plane tickets to allow them flexibility on expeditions like this one. Problem was, I didn't have any flexibility, because I had to be back for the start of the next term's classes, and I also had to get there using frequent-flier miles, since I couldn't afford to buy the plane ticket. The only ticket I could get using my airline miles departed within an hour of my last scheduled final exam, which was for my least favorite class—Derivatives. That meant I would have to race through my test in order to make my flight.

Derivatives class was hard. At least it was for me, because I didn't have any finance background when I entered the MBA program at Duke. Truth be told, final exams in all the quantitative classes were difficult for me. What made it worse was when my classmates would say things to me like, "Business school is *so* boring because it's *so* easy." I'd look astonished and then try to recover: "Oh, um, yeah. I know..." *Yawn. Stretch.* Really? I wanted to hit them with my fancy new calculator—the one that had formulas for sta-tistics, cash flows, depreciation business percentages, bond math, and other stuff—*which I had absolutely no idea how to use*. I struggled much of the time in graduate school. Many of my classmates had finance backgrounds and/or were CPAs. As a liberal arts major in college, I had never even taken a basic accounting class. I was pretty certain that when it came to the quant stuff, I was one of the dumber people in our class. I envied my classmates who generally seemed to sail through the coursework. You always knew who the smartest students in the class were because they were the suck-ups. Wait—I mean, because they were really good about participating in class. They were the ones whose hands always shot up with "pick me pick me" lightning speed whenever the professor asked a question. And they *loved* exam day. They were the first ones to get out of their seats, walk up to the professor's desk, and enthusiastically hand over their finished exams as if they were delivering a Publishers Clearing House check to a family of eight who had been surviving on food stamps.

This one time, I beat them to it. I was the first person to finish the exam, which was huge for me, because I was usually one of the last people sitting in the classroom racing against the clock to finish. Not today—the day of my flight to Jakarta (which was the starting point for my expedition). I got out of my chair before anyone else did, walked down to the front of the room, and proudly dropped my exam paper in front of my professor. Everyone looked up in amazement when they saw me hand in my exam—somewhat surprised that I was done first, only because I was typically fairly quiet in class, and (as everyone knows) the quiet ones usually don't understand the lecture material. As I walked out of the classroom I paused at the door and gave my classmates a look over my shoulder like, *I can't believe you guys are still working on that test. I'm finished.*

In fact, the material was so far over my head that I knew I would probably fail the exam whether I sat there for three hours or thirty hours, so I decided to cut my losses. I finished the first page of a six-page exam, left the rest of it blank, and walked out the door. Sitting there for another two hours wasn't going to bring me any closer to solving the exam problems that were staring me down. Besides, I had a mountain to climb.

Carstensz Pyramid is located north of Australia in what was then known as Irian Jaya—the western part of Papua New Guinea. Western New Guinea was a Dutch territory until the early 1960s, when Indonesia stepped in and took control. Irian Jaya was none too happy about this as they wanted independence, so war and violence ensued as the locals organized a separatist movement in an attempt to gain freedom. The clashes have been ongoing for decades, and as of 2013 more than 150,000 people have been killed. As a result of the civil unrest and violence, the entire area was closed off to tourism for many years. But I thought to myself, *Why let a little rebel activity spoil my fall break from grad school?* I had a Swiss Army knife—the really big one—with the toothpick and the tweezers. And the mini magnifying glass.

While I knew it wasn't the brightest idea to go over there by myself, I couldn't afford to join a guided expedition—those were running about $6,000 to $8,000 at the time (the fees are more like $18,000 to $20,000 these days).

So I organized the trip on my own by corresponding with a local logistics coordinator in Indonesia named Monty, who claimed that he could arrange local transportation and guides for Carstensz Pyramid. I found Monty's contact information on the Internet, but this was long before the days of Google or Wikipedia—back when an online search still required a lot of effort. I did quite a bit of digging, but other than an e-mail address and phone number I found basically no information about Monty and Co.—and with no Yelp or Angie's List, I had no way of knowing how reliable or unreliable he might be. But he claimed he could arrange a permit for me so I decided to trust him. And besides, he was the only lead I had at that point, so I really had no choice.

Very few people had climbed Carstensz Pyramid, in part because it's so hard to get to it. The peak lies deep in a densely forested jungle. On top of that, the mountain had technically been closed to climbers since 1995 due to the civil unrest in the region, so the 411 was pretty limited. Monty quoted me an initial cost of $800, which sounded pretty good. He also said that if I brought him two Suunto altimeter watches from the United States, he would knock the price down even further. Deal.

I made my plane, and sixty thousand frequent-flier miles later I arrived in Jakarta. I found my way to the hotel where I was to connect with Monty. I settled in and tried calling him—no luck. His phone rang and rang—there was no answer, and no answering machine or voice mail. But I knew Monty would contact me at some point, because I had the altimeter watches he wanted, so I wasn't too concerned. Monty finally called and left a message at my hotel saying he would come by the following afternoon to meet with me. I breathed a huge sigh of relief.

While strolling through the hotel lobby, I ran into a few others who had also arranged trips through Monty, so at least I knew he was for real (or if he wasn't, then I wouldn't be the only fool who had fallen for his scam). The other people who would be heading to the mountain with me were Jaime Viñals from Guatemala, Harry Kikstra from Holland, José Mijares from Spain, and Mark Gunlogson, a guide from the adventure travel company Mountain Madness (he later became its president and owner). Mark was there with a private client, Joe Wolfgruber.

There were also some climbers from Poland at the hotel who had arranged their climb through Monty. The Polish team was comprised of some of the world's best mountaineers, including Leszek Cichy, who made history when he successfully completed the first-ever winter ascent of Mount Everest with Krzysztof Wielicki in 1980. That climb was the first winter ascent of *any* 8,000-meter peak, so it was epic and still stands as one of the greatest feats in mountaineering. Cichy was hoping to summit Carstensz and thus become the first Polish climber to complete the Seven Summits.

Anna Czerwińska was also part of the team. She is one of the world's most accomplished female climbers, having summited multiple 8,000-meter peaks, including Everest. She also made headlines as part of the first team of women to climb the North Face of the Matterhorn in winter. She was well-known in the climbing community, and if successful on Carstensz, she would become the first Polish woman to complete the Seven Summits. A couple of the Polish team members had come off an Everest expedition four months earlier, so needless to say this group was in tip-top shape. I was in awe of my new Polish climbing companions and was eager to make conversation, but their group seemed to speak little English. And I knew even less Polish. "Krzyzewski" was about it for me.

The next day we all finally met Monty, who showed up at our hotel to update us on the situation. Unfortunately, our climbing permits had not cleared. So there I was, sitting in a hotel lobby in Jakarta trying to negotiate my way to a mountain that was right smack in the center of a region that had been plagued by violence for more than three decades.

Monty was adamant. "I'm sorry, but you cannot go climb the mountain. It is impossible. Irian Jaya is not safe, and the area surrounding the mountain has been shut down. No one can pass through there anymore."

I, too, was adamant. "What do you mean I can't go? I just used sixty thousand frequent-flier miles to get here!"

Monty explained that because of the civil war in the region there was no way to get to the base of the mountain. The separatist uprisings and violence had been getting progressively worse, and the death toll was climbing in recent months despite intervention from the International Committee of the Red Cross and other humanitarian organizations. And Carstensz was right smack in the middle of the rebel activity.

I looked around at the other climbers. They were as discouraged as I was. Many of them had already been waiting for weeks for the violence in the area to subside so that their permits would clear. I didn't have weeks. I only had a few days. So there I was, sitting on the floor of the hotel lobby with nine other climbers, hoping someone had an answer. No one did. At that point it looked as if I had wasted my entire bank of frequent-flier miles as well as my fall break from graduate school. I leaned forward and put my head down on the ground and wondered how the hell I had gotten myself into this situation. Monty told us to be patient.

Then…the God of separatist movements smiled down upon us. Two days after Monty had delivered the bad news, our permits cleared. Score! But there was a footnote: we would have to wait a few days to leave for the climb. The area was still very dangerous, so we would need the Indonesian Army to escort us through the jungle, and it would take some time to organize those gentlemen.

Monty also introduced us to Rudi Nurcahyo, a local Indonesian guide who would be taking us to the mountain. Rudi had a warm smile and a pleasant demeanor. He spoke pretty decent English and was himself an Everest veteran from the 1997 Indonesian Everest Expedition. I noticed Rudi's handshake felt a little odd, and when I looked down I saw that he had no fingers on his right hand (he was missing one on his left, too). Turns out he'd lost them to frostbite on Aconcagua in 1992. Within the first five minutes of meeting Rudi I could tell two things: (1) he was probably going to be a pretty good guide, and (2) he probably sucked at Rock-Paper-Scissors.

I was ecstatic. We were going to the mountain. But wait... *not so fast*. One more barrier shot up in front of us. The Indonesian presidential elections had just taken place, and now there was chaos in Jakarta. Thousands of people were protesting the election results. So now it wasn't just Irian Jaya that was a mess; Jakarta was a mess, too. There were literally riots in the streets. Local businesses shut down as shop owners boarded up their windows to thwart vandals and looters. The violence escalated to the point where the airport was under siege, and no planes were landing or taking off, so our flight to Irian Jaya was delayed *again*. My timing for this trip could not have been worse.

The authorities were telling people to stay off the streets. But I was going stir-crazy and was getting hungry and was sick of the hotel's food. There was actually a Sizzler down the street and it was calling my name—loud enough for me to hear it over the screaming protesters who had flooded the city's public spaces. I peered out the window of my hotel room. People were yelling and turning over cars and smashing windows and setting things on fire. But I wasn't scared.

I had been to Oakland Raiders games (and had survived). I finally decided I had to venture out to get something to eat.

I left the hotel and made the several-block journey down the street to the Sizzler on foot and without incident. I was absolutely elated to be inside an American franchise restaurant. There was something familiar about it (menu boards with pictures of food that I actually recognized), which brightened my mood. I wanted to spend as much time there as I could, because there was nowhere else to go other than back to the hotel room. I chewed every bite of my steak about fifty times to make it last (well, and because it was so rubbery that it was the only way I could get it down).

Then, as I was on the forty-seventh chew of my third-to-last bite of steak, the noises outside began getting louder. It was the protesters. They were obviously getting closer and closer. The manager of the Sizzler ran to the front of the restaurant in a panic and closed some iron gates across the front doors and windows in an attempt to safeguard the restaurant. I was locked inside as the protesters rallied in the streets. I heard screaming, yelling, and gunfire. My thought was this: if you are going to get locked inside a building, it's best to do so in a place that has an all-you-can-eat dessert bar. After polishing off about twelve sundaes, I decided to brave the streets of Jakarta and venture back toward my hotel.

Back safe and sound in the hotel, I now had to face the fact that the delays of the past few days had put my climb in jeopardy. I didn't have that much time left to get to the mountain, climb it, and get back to North Carolina in time for the start of classes. I was on a partial scholarship, and I was worried that if I didn't register on time for the next term, I might lose my financial aid. The problem now was that even if we were to leave immediately for Irian Jaya, I would only have two days to get to base camp and climb. I had the option of getting my money refunded and heading back for classes, *or* getting on a plane to Irian Jaya and trying to do the climb in forty-eight hours. Bear in mind that the schedule normally allotted six days for the actual climb, to allow for acclimatization and weather (the rest of the time on the ten-day schedule was designated for air travel).

I thought about cutting my losses and going home, but that thought quickly vanished. I knew there was no way I was going to go home without getting to that mountain. I decided to see how far I could go in two days.

Well, with the help of the Indonesian Army we were finally able to fly to Irian Jaya and start our trek through the jungle. The walk to the base of Carstensz Pyramid was like something out of a movie. I found it all fascinating. First we had to pass through the Grasberg mine—the largest gold mine in the world. The mine is majority-owned by Freeport-McMoRan. It's also the subject of considerable controversy, including allegations that the firm has engaged in human rights abuses and that its mining operations have inflicted enormous environmental damage. After we made our way through the mine we entered the dense jungle, where we experienced torrential downpours and met people the likes of whom I had never seen.

The region is home to hundreds of different tribes—but the majority of the people we passed during the trek were from the Dani tribe. Rudi explained that most of them had never seen white people before, so as we passed by their groups I wasn't entirely sure whether or not it would be appropriate to reach out and shake their hands. I was, however, 100 percent sure that whatever the local custom might call for (and said local custom was a mystery to me), I wasn't going to reach out and shake anyone's *koteka* (that's a penis gourd, a spectacularly showy device worn by the Dani tribesmen for reasons that are obscure to me).

We eventually made it to base camp. What's more, we did it *without a single murder or kidnapping or riot along the way*. I felt pretty good upon arrival at 14,000 feet, although I knew going from sea level to 16,000 feet in two days would be no picnic. While I had been to much higher altitudes, I had never ascended that fast. Even on nontechnical climbs like Mount Kilimanjaro, you start at 6,600 feet and you typically never gain more than 3,300 to 3,900 feet of elevation in a day. This was a whole different deal, though, as it would be a fast ascent that required basic rock-climbing skills at altitude. But I figured I was ready. *Game on.* The plan was to spend the next day at base camp, and then head up the mountain the following morning at zero dark thirty.

I didn't sleep at all the following night—which, as I've mentioned, is pretty normal just before a summit attempt like this. You know you have to get up before dawn to get ready to leave, so you toss and turn and look at your watch every ten minutes to make sure you haven't slept through the alarm. I didn't have to worry about sleeping through my watch alarm; not only did the sound of the nonstop torrential downpour keep me awake, but I also couldn't seem to get warm in my sleeping bag, which was weird because my bag was rated for twenty below, and it couldn't have been colder than forty degrees. I sat up and felt around the tent for my headlamp—and at that point I realized there was a leak in the tent and everything was completely soaked: my sleeping bag, my fleece jacket and fleece pants (which I had been using as a pillow). Pretty much everything I had with me was wet. This is the kind of thing you might laugh about

Stone memorials honoring fallen climbers can be seen at Dugla Pass on the way to Everest base camp, a sobering reminder of the dangers inherent in mountaineering.
(Alison Levine)

Passing by the memorial for Scott Fischer, one of America's top climbers, who died while guiding a group on Everest in 1996.
(Jake Norton for Discovery Communications)

Summit 29,029'
LHOTSE
NUPTSE
26,300'
Camp IV
Camp III 24,000'
EVEREST
21,000' Camp II
Camp I 19,500'
Base Camp
Khumbu Icefall
17,600'

South Col/ Southeast Ridge route on Mount Everest.
(Alpine Ascents International)

Everest base camp at sunset.   *(Jake Norton for Discovery Communications)*

Sherpas building the *puja* altar at base camp, an important part of the ritual performed before expedition members proceed up the mountain.   *(Alison Levine)*

The first American Women's Everest Expedition with big smiles at Everest base camp. From left to right: Kim Clark, Lynn Prebble, Midge Cross, Jody Thompson, and me. (*Jake Norton for Discovery Communications*)

The women pose with a team of Sherpas—the true heroes of Mount Everest. (*Jake Norton for Discovery Communications*)

Ford's promotional piece for the 2003 Ford Expedition. (*Eric Perry*)

Tents at Camp 1 on Everest (19,500 feet). *(Garret Madison)*

American Women's Everest Expedition approaching Camp 4, in the death zone.
(Jake Norton for Discovery Communications)

American Women's Everest Expedition at the South Summit in 2002.
(*Jake Norton for Discovery Communications*)

A glimpse of the dangers of the Khumbu Icefall on the south side of Everest. *(Jake Norton for Discovery Communications)*

Me, crossing a crevasse in 2002.
(Jake Norton for Discovery Communications)

That's me going through the Icefall in 2010. You can see the fixed lines that climbers use to increase their chances of surviving a fall should the ice suddenly shift or collapse under them. *(Don Healy)*

Climbers in the Khumbu Icefall just below Camp 1. *(Garrett Madison)*

Some handy camera work from my friend Jake Norton, a talented climber and photographer. *(Jake Norton for Discovery Communications)*

Seven ladders strung together at 20,000 feet in the Khumbu Icefall. *(Alpine Ascents Archives)*

The Ilyushin 76 that carried us from Chile to Antarctica.   *(Alison Levine)*

After landing on the Antarctic continent, we took a ski-equipped Twin Otter to the edge of the Ronne Ice Shelf.   *(Alison Levine)*

My polar look.
(Eric Philips, Icetrek®)

Dragging my sled, en route to the South Pole.
(Eric Philips, Icetrek®)

My tent and my skis, buried in snow in the middle of Antarctica. My sled is in the foreground, barely visible.
(Alison Levine)

Team CAN DU at the South Pole. From left to right (back row): me, Bernice Notenboom, Merete Spilling Gjertsen, George Szwender. Eric Philips is crouching down in front. *(Eric Philips, Icetrek®)*

Hanging out with the locals prior to the trek to Carstensz base camp. *(Alison Levine)*

Many of the local Dani tribesmen still wear *kotekas* (penis gourds). *(Jaime Viñals)*

At the summit of Carstensz Pyramid in 1999. *(Alison Levine)*

My Gore-Tex pants. Or what was left of them after the Carstensz climb. *(Alison Levine)*

With fellow Thayer Leader Development Group advisor Brig. Gen. (Ret.) Pete Dawkins. *(Alison Levine)*

The amazing Meg
Berté Owen.
*(Copyright Bristol-
Myers Squibb, 2005)*

Meg's name
engraved on my
ice axe.
(Alison Levine)

Spike, the Gonzaga
Bulldogs' mascot—
brought to Mount
Everest by my climbing
partner John Rudolph—
is shown here in a
photo, courtesy of
the FBI. Spike was
kidnapped, bound,
and gagged. He was
later released but was
missing an ear.

Receiving a good luck blessing from seventy-nine-year-old Lama Geshe during the approach to Everest base camp in 2010. *(Alison Levine)*

Mount Everest on a clear day. If only my summit day had looked like this! *(Garrett Madison)*

Everest Camp 4 at the South Col (26,300 feet). *(Garrett Madison)*

Summit Ridge on Everest. Visibility during my summit attempt was very poor. *(Garrett Madison)*

That's me (middle, in blue) at 28,740 feet, ascending the Hillary Step. *(Brad Jackson)*

May 24, 2010, at the summit of Mount Everest—8,848 meters, 29,029 feet. This was the final summit needed to complete the Adventure Grand Slam. *(Alison Levine)*

Shadow of Everest's summit. This image reminds me that there will always be more mountains to climb, so I must continue to strive to be better. *(Jake Norton for Discovery Communications)*

Back at sea level with Trooper. *(Alison Levine)*

if you were sharing a tent with someone, but somehow it's never quite as funny when you are solo and there is no one to commiserate with.

So what else could go wrong? Well, for starters, aliens invaded my stomach. I started feeling pains right after dinner, and they got progressively worse. I lay there in my tent praying the pains would stop. No dice. I had taken a bunch of Imodium, but whatever was in my gut just laughed and mainlined it. I couldn't keep anything inside me. There was no way I could climb. I couldn't even stand up at that point.

At about 2:00 a.m. everyone rolled out of their tents and got ready to head up. I could see their headlamps shining outside my tent, and I felt disappointment seeping into my tent along with the rain. But I wasn't ready to give up yet. I told the group to go ahead and that I would be behind them by just a few minutes, although I knew realistically it would be much longer than that. Rudi (the only English-speaking local with our group) took off with the Polish team and the other climbers, but before he went he asked one of the army soldiers, Eres, to wait behind and climb with me when I was ready to head out. Eres was also eager to head up the mountain, and I'm guessing he wasn't thrilled that he had been asked to split from the rest of the group (safety in numbers). But he was incredibly gracious about the whole thing—or at least he had a gracious look on his face. He didn't speak any English, so who really knows apart from Eres himself?

Meanwhile, I still couldn't seem to keep any food or liquids inside me. I knew I needed to head out soon if I was going to go at all. This was the only window I had to try to go up, since I had to be back down the next day in order to hike out in time to catch my flight home. But my stomach didn't seem to want to cooperate.

Here I feel the need to point out that an upset stomach (what a euphemism that is) is no fun when you're lying around your house in sweatpants and have a clean toilet and running water nearby. But when you are in the middle of a jungle…well, let's just say it's even more of a bummer. Then add four layers of clothing and a climbing harness and fingers that are not exactly nimble in the cold temperatures, and you've got a "challenging situation." Nightmare. Yeah. Total nightmare. Even water sent my stomach into a Cirque du Soleil routine.

So, instead of the normal superhydration and carbo-loading mode that climbers go into prior to a summit bid, I decided not eat or drink anything (including water) for the next several hours. And while my normal routine on most climbs is to stop every hour to drink and eat something, I knew that this time such fueling stops were not going to be an option. If I wanted to climb this mountain, I'd have to climb it on empty. I had climbed when my body had been calorie depleted in the past, and I had a good idea of how far I could push it. I knew that if or when I hit the wall, I would need to turn around. I would make that call when the time came, if it came. But for now, I wanted to at least *try*.…

The next eighteen hours were, to put it mildly, full of surprises. Let's start with the fact that I didn't anticipate the summit bid taking eighteen hours. I knew I would be low on energy and would move slowly as a result, and that I would need to stop frequently to "take care of business." But I figured the climb would take me ten hours at most. Carstensz Pyramid is the only one of the Seven Summits that requires rock-climbing skills, but much of the route has fixed lines, which means climbers can ascend and descend efficiently. And while I was comfortable with the climbing,

I had not anticipated the shoddy (by which I mean scary-looking) anchors and the ropes that were often too fat to fit through my gear. Standard ascending and descending gear (with fancy names such as jumars or ascenders or ATCs or figure 8s) were no good on many of the ropes. I managed to make a friction knot (called a Prusik knot) out of some nylon cord to help me ascend the steeper pitches, but it was still sketchy.

I moved along the route slowly. I was making decent time, although I was several hours behind the rest of the group. When I was about two-thirds of the way to the top, my new climbing buddies loomed into sight on their way back down from the summit. I high-fived them as they passed me (this was back in '99, so the fist bump wasn't around yet) and plastered a fake smile on my face and acted as if I felt okay. But I didn't. Due to my GI troubles I was really too weak to be climbing at altitude. A voice in my head suggested that I turn back right there and descend with them because it would be safer for me to be with a group in case anything went wrong—but the voice wasn't loud enough or maybe it was in broken English or something, because I didn't bother to listen. I continued to climb, with Eres right behind me. I reached the summit after about ten hours of climbing. Eres and I took a few photos at the top and then began the journey back down. I was so excited to be at the top, but I reminded myself that (say it with me) the summit was merely the halfway point of my climb. I still needed to get back down.

At this point, the clouds closed in and it started to snow. Then my Raynaud's decided to kick in, so the nerves in my fingers and toes clamped down on the blood vessels, cutting off my circulation. My hands were now numb to the point where I had very little dexterity. No worries: I'd brought two sets of hand warmers and had only used one on the way up. I busted out the second one and waited for it to warm up so that I could regain the use of my hands. I waited. And waited. And waited. It never warmed up. It was defective.

Mistake #1: I didn't bring enough sets of hand warmers. My fingers turned completely white and I couldn't move them, which made it really hard to work the ropes and other gear that I needed to descend the exposed parts of the route. Every pitch was scary. Every single one.

It was now getting late and I was losing the sun. My prescription sunglasses were now too dark to wear at this point.

Mistake #2: leaving my regular prescription glasses behind. I didn't bring my regular glasses because it was light out when I started the ascent, and I was sure I would be off the mountain loooooong before nightfall. Alas, I had greatly misjudged the amount of time it would take me to get to the summit and back. Now, in the growing darkness, I couldn't really see the route ahead of me. And actually, once the sun completely disappeared, I could not even see the ground in front of me.

I was moving very slowly now. More than fifteen hours of climbing had burned through whatever calories I hadn't expelled from my body, so I had no energy. I couldn't move my fingers. I couldn't see very well. I was freezing, and it was getting colder as night descended on the peak. Many parts of the descent were totally exposed and unprotected. You fall, you go all the way down. Hundreds of feet. Maybe a thousand. I didn't know. I couldn't see where the lower ledges were. I dug through my backpack to get my headlamp, which I actually *did* bring (even though I did not expect to be climbing in the dark), because it never leaves the top section of my backpack. It's always in there. That, and toilet paper. I learned early in my climbing career (which at that time spanned about a year) to always, *always* keep a head-lamp with me.

I strapped the headlamp onto my climbing helmet and flipped the switch on. Nothing. No worries—I had a spare battery. So I swapped bad for good…and still nothing. It wasn't a bad battery; it was a burned-out *bulb*. And I didn't have another one of those with me—which was, of course, Mistake #3.

Now I *really* couldn't see anything. Eres was right there with me on the descent, but his headlamp wasn't all that great (although it was better than no headlamp). I got down on my butt and scooted across many of the ridges, because I could not see where I was stepping and the route was so damn steep. I don't think I have ever been so scared. Truly scared, to the point that I could barely breathe. I slammed my knees against rocks a couple of times, and eventually I smacked into something hard with just about every other part of my body. I was too tired to scream obscenities (or anything at all) and too dehydrated to cry. A kind of numb-ness set in. I tried to just focus on my next step. I tried to concentrate on breathing normally. I would have given any-thing to be back at base camp, in the comfort of the kitchen tent with the other climbers and our army escorts, downing some hot tea and a plate of chicken feet.

Spoiler alert: Eres and I made it back to base camp. It was late in the evening. I was drenched. (It was pouring rain lower down the mountain—too much rain even for my Gore-Tex jacket—and I had ripped the seat of my water-proof pants on the way down, so all of my layers were soaked through.) I was freezing, since my body did not have enough energy to generate any warmth, and my fingers and toes were completely numb. My head and my knees were throbbing. I was hungry and severely dehydrated—thanks to my GI issues, it had now been more than twenty-four hours since I'd had any food or water. I was grateful that it was dark so that no one could see the pathetic state I was in as I stumbled into base camp. I fell into my tent and tried to sleep, but I was so cold I couldn't stop shaking for hours.

The next morning I awoke to voices outside my tent. I opened the zipper and emerged from my little nylon house. I didn't understand what they were saying, but the Polish climbers were standing there looking at my torn-up pants, which were laid across the rocks next to my tent. They were smiling and chuckling as they picked up my pants to assess the damage. They even took a picture of them as I held them up. I could tell by the looks on their faces that they figured out that my climb was "eventful." They shook my hand and patted me on the back. It wasn't a winter ascent of Everest, but it was epic, and I appreciated that they appreciated this fact.

Harry, José, Mark, and Jaime came over to my tent and gave me hugs. Rudi was busy cooking breakfast, but I'm sure he would have given me a thumbs-up if he had been there (and had a thumb). We all sat down together in the kitchen tent, and I began to tell them my story, although the various bruises covering my body could have told the story without my words. I had made it to the summit and back, but I knew I could have easily *not* made it back, and it was genuinely frightening to contemplate that fact.

I barely made it home to North Carolina in time for the first day of classes for the new term. I hadn't read any of the course material, so I was completely unprepared. When the professors asked questions I would raise my hand, pretending as if I had the answer, and then when they called on me I would go into a seemingly uncontrollable coughing fit and frantically clutch my throat and pretend as if I suddenly couldn't talk. I looked around at my classmates with that rueful *I so wish I could answer this one and share my knowledge with all of you, but sadly, I am unable to speak* look on my (pathetic) face.

While I did come back in one piece, my Gore-Tex pants—the most expensive clothing item I owned—were completely trashed. They were covered in mud, and the entire seat was ripped out. I couldn't afford a new pair, because I had already run through my budget paying off Monty and the Indonesian Army. The ridiculous thing is that if I had just brought my glasses and a spare headlamp bulb the morning I left for the summit, I wouldn't have ruined a $250 pair of pants! But I hadn't, so now I needed a new pair.

Then I remembered—I was pretty sure that North Face products carried a lifetime warranty. I checked their website and confirmed that they will repair or replace their products if there are defects in material or workmanship. The warranty stated: "Even after extended use, we'll repair the product without charge, or replace it at our discretion." Good enough. I marched my mud-covered pants with the ripped-out *ss to the North Face store. I walked up to the first salesperson I saw and sheepishly said, "Uh, I need to return some pants because they have a defect." The guy asked, "What kind of defect?" "They have a hole in them," I answered. "So I need to swap them for a pair that doesn't have any holes."

I then held up what was left of my black Gore-Tex pants, which were caked in dried mud and had multiple rips and tears. The guy looked at me and gave my pants the once-over and said, "Are those *our* pants?" Of course he didn't recognize them as North Face pants because they didn't look anything like they did when I originally bought them. Hell, they were barely recognizable as *pants*.

I couldn't look him in the face. I stared at the ground and mumbled, "Yes. They are your pants—these are most definitely North Face pants. I bought them in this store last year and, uh...I would like to return them because there is a big hole in them—riiiiiiight...here!" I pointed to the gaping hole where the backside of the pants used to be.

He looked at me, looked at the pants, looked back at me again—square in the eye—and squinted as he spoke while trying to keep a straight face. "Yeah...but that doesn't really look like a manufacturing defect." I looked up at him with my best clueless facial expression as if he were speaking a foreign language. He continued. "That damage looks like it was man-made."

I went straight to my best *I have absolutely no idea what you are talking about* look and then seamlessly transitioned to my *shocked beyond belief that you would say that* expression. "Huh? *Man-made?* Nope. No way. This damage was definitely *not* man-made." I tried to sound even more convincing.

He looked a little puzzled. "Really, you are telling me that the damage to these Gore-Tex pants—or what used to be a pair of pants—*wasn't* man-made?!?!?" His eyes were enough to call me out. I knew his bullsh*t meter was registering off the charts.

But God, I needed him to give me a new pair of pants. "No. It wasn't. I swear!" I looked him in the eye for the first time and confidently announced, "It was *woman-made*."

He smiled and said, "I gotta hear the story."

He must have liked it, because he gave me a new pair of pants.

Carstensz Pyramid isn't a superhigh or a superhard peak, but I still got my *ss handed to me. Many incredibly skilled climbers have died on much lower mountains because they didn't have the proper equipment. It's easy to think, *Oh, I won't need that,* or *It's too much of a hassle to carry the extra weight,* or *I bet someone else will bring one of those, so I'll leave mine behind.* If and when those thoughts arrive, I strongly urge you to think again.

People tend to let mistakes slide when the errors are made by someone who is new to a job or a pursuit or even a project. But the "I didn't know any better" excuse doesn't work for people in leadership positions. As a leader, it's your job, even when new to a particular role, to know what you need in order to achieve a particular goal. That means doing the research, putting in the preparation time, and showing up with the right stuff. What's the right stuff? It's whatever you need to get the job done on time and in a way that allows you to stand tall and be proud of your results.

When I set out to climb Carstensz Pyramid I was willing to do whatever it took to get to the summit. I had blown a final exam, burned through all of my frequent-flier miles, survived violent political protests and rebel uprisings, trekked through a jungle with the Indonesian Army, and made it to the base of a remote and rarely climbed mountain with some of the world's most accomplished climbers...and then almost blew my chances of coming back from the expedition in one piece because some pieces of important gear got left back at base camp. Someone screwed up, and I place 100 percent of the blame on the expedition leader—*and that leader was me.* You are always your own designated leader. You may or may not have someone with an official leadership title with you on a climb or on the job, but you are always responsible for your own preparation, your performance, and your outcomes.

One last thing: if you think you can't afford all the gear you need, ask yourself if you can afford to *not* have it. You can bet that your competitors are investing in the best and most advanced technology available; you need to do the same. Don't put yourself or your team at a disadvantage because you didn't bother to get the proper equipment. Sure, there is something charming about old-school—but while the mountaineers in the 1800s looked dapper as they climbed in their tweed suits and leather hobnailed boots, it's much better to be climbing in lightweight, weatherproof clothing and insulated boots with crampons in the twenty-first century.

I know some folks who didn't have the best equipment on their first expedition to Everest and didn't make it to the top. On their second attempt they invested in better gear—including newer, lighter oxygen tanks, which allowed them to move faster on summit day and enabled them to tag the top.

There are always going to be ways to get whatever it is you need at a price you can afford, if you are willing to put some time into looking. When I started climbing, eBay didn't exist, but I was able to borrow some items that I needed (and didn't have) from friends. What really saved me was finding a secondhand store in Seattle that had a pair of extra-small down pants that I knew would fit me and were one-sixth the price of a new pair.

There is no excuse for not having the proper equipment. "I can't afford it" isn't a good reason. What you can't afford is to show up for duty unprepared and without the right gear. Think of a football player showing up for a game without a helmet. Or a boxer stepping into the ring without his gloves. Or a golfer showing up without clubs. Leaders need tools, too—the tools to survive, the tools to thrive, and the tools to help the people around them achieve their goals.

By the way, I failed my Derivatives exam—which didn't surprise me, since I left five-sixths of the exam blank. Somehow I still managed to pass the class. Barely. I received a warning letter from the associate dean informing me that if it happened again I could be placed on academic probation. So was it worth it? You bet.

File under "Bring the Right Stuff"

You are responsible for knowing what tools you need to get the job done and for making sure that your team is properly equipped. Make sure you have the right stuff. "I didn't know" and "I can't afford it" aren't valid excuses. When you show up, ready to take on a challenge, you'd better *bring it*.

Chapter 8

YOU'RE NOT SPECIAL

Building Trust and Loyalty

There's a lot of pressure toward the end of an Everest expedition. All of your hard work during your time on the mountain's slopes (not to mention the months or *years* of preparation you put in before even getting to the mountain) is going to either pay off or blow up on *one final day*—and, as I have mentioned numerous times, whether you get to the tippy-top or not is often decided by things that are totally out of your control. It's not fair. Well, tell it to the Mountain Gods.

I have heard people say that your performance on summit day is the only thing that matters. Not true. What you do *every day* matters. Including the way you treat others—which is something you can absolutely control, regardless of what environment you happen to be in. Never discount the value of courtesy and compassion when it comes to achieving a goal, especially when the going gets rough. In other words, *be nice*. The only people who can get away with not being nice are those who are really, really good at what they do. Damn good.

When you're exceptionally talented, people tend to overlook your personality flaws and extreme quirkiness in light of your performance. But if you are not a superstar, you better darn well be nice, otherwise no one is going to put up with you. It's that simple. You can be mediocre and nice, or you can be great and be an *sshole. But you cannot be a mediocre *sshole.

Look at NBA player Dennis Rodman—no, don't look at the fines he has paid for fighting with other players and kicking cameramen during games, don't look at his outrageous appearance or foul mouth, or even his stint on *Celebrity Rehab with Dr. Drew*. Look at his *stats*. Rodman—who was controversial because of his behavior—was one of the most talented defensive players ever to grace the hardwood. He played on five NBA championship teams and despite the fact that he was only six foot seven (not particularly tall in NBA-land) he led the NBA in rebounds per game for seven straight years. In 2011, he was inducted into the Naismith Memorial Basketball Hall of Fame.

NBA coach Phil Jackson called Rodman the greatest athlete he ever coached, which is saying *a lot*, because Jackson also coached celebrated players Michael Jordan, Kobe Bryant, and Shaquille O'Neal. In a speech delivered to the University of North Dakota, Jackson said of Rodman, "He could probably play a forty-eight-minute game and play the forty-eighth minute stronger than the first minute of the game....He was that terrific an athlete." While Rodman was well-known for his tantrums and antics both on and off the court, he got away with his behavior because he was *that good*.

But imagine what would happen to a mediocre player who behaved that way: his team would turn on him, the fans would turn on him, and the league would turn on him. Here's the deal: if you can't rebound like Rodman, you have to make up for it in charm and personality. And I don't mean in a "stand-up comedy" kind of way (although a sense of humor never hurts). I'm talking about being selfless and gracious and having a positive attitude.

Don't ever underestimate the importance of treating others with respect and kindness. I know a climber who left an Everest expedition early not because he was sick, not because he was injured, not because he had a family emergency at home, but because he was just struggling with the climb and was unable to perform at a level that ensured his safety. Unfortunately he was told by his guides that he could not continue on the expedition that season; his climb was ending early.

What does this have to do with being nice? This: he wasn't the worst climber in his group from a strength perspective—and he definitely had an abundance of willpower. The problem was his attitude. In extreme environments, a bad attitude can be dangerous. Not just in terms of morale, but in terms of putting your life, or the lives of others, at risk.

This fellow would routinely leave critical pieces of gear or clothing behind because he didn't want to carry the extra weight. Of course when he arrived at the next camp he wouldn't have what he needed, and then his guides or others in his group had to lend him their own clothing and equipment to ensure his safety. It wasn't like he was *accidentally* forgetting things; he just didn't want to add the extra weight to his pack, and he expected others to pick up his slack.

Although he received a great deal of coaching and a steady flow of suggestions on how he might remedy some of the issues he was struggling with, he didn't seem amenable to changing his ways. And despite the favors others in his group continued to do for him (carrying weight for him and lending him their gear), he showed no appreciation. He ended up quitting the climb. Leaving the expedition two-thirds of the way into it was not his choice; the guides were the ones who sent him packing. On Everest, the permit holder (in this case, his lead guide) controls who has access to the upper part of the mountain. Climbers can be sent home because of a lack of preparedness or an inability to climb safely—or any other reason that jeopardizes their safety or the well-being of their team.

His guides sent him home because they didn't want him to injure himself—or anyone else. But I don't think that was the only reason they pulled the plug on his trip. Yes, there were issues with skill level, but some coaching could have fixed that. Certainly less skilled people have made it up the mountain. The fact that he constantly clashed with others (who were doing their best to help him) played a huge part in the decision to send him home. He was unable to follow directions, and he became angry and combative when anyone tried to give him advice. He continued his abusive behavior patterns, which pretty much ended the trip for him—because in extreme environments, one team member's actions can affect everyone else's safety. While he had much more experience than many other people on the mountain, he still wasn't able to master the basic practices that are compulsory for safe climbing on Mount

Everest, *because he simply refused to listen*. Pretty rough for him emotionally to have had to call it quits. But hopes are dashed and dreams are crushed on the mountain every day. There isn't a lot of room for error, and safety trumps all.

I *do* think if this guy had shown more effort toward correcting the mistakes he was consistently making, he may have been allowed to continue on the climb. Had he been able to take constructive criticism and implement advice, and had he been more courteous to those who were trying to help him instead of becoming defensive and angry, perhaps things could have gone differently. How we treat people is always our choice, and if we choose not to be respectful, it can come back to bite us.

Here's a very different story about a climber who also struggled through an Everest expedition and also ended up with an unexpected early departure. I've purposely changed some of the names and details about people throughout this book in order to create some anonymity, but there are certain characters who should not remain anonymous: John Rudolph (JR) and I were constantly at odds throughout the trip in 2010. Every night during dinner we would argue nonstop. See, JR knew college basketball *almost* as well as I did. And he was just as passionate about it. Problem was, he was a huge Gonzaga fan. *Huge.*

Every night I had to listen to him brag about his beloved Gonzaga Bulldogs (I mean, really . . .). He even had a miniature stuffed animal with him on the climb—Spike, the Gonzaga Bulldogs' mascot.

Side note: There was a very unfortunate incident at base camp where someone kidnapped Spike, duct-taped his mouth shut, bound his little paws behind his back, and then this sicko cut off poor Spike's ear à la *Reservoir Dogs* and left the bloody ear wrapped up in a ransom note demanding one million dollars in exchange for Spike's safe return (some people believed the blood to be ketchup that was swiped from the mess tent, but trust me–it was *real blood*!). I have no idea who would do such a twisted thing. The only clue we had about the perpetrator was he or she possessed a roll of bright pink duct tape (as this was used to cover Spike's mouth), but other than that, there were no solid leads. To this day the crime remains unsolved.

Anyway, JR ended up having a hard time on the trip due to some pretty severe health problems; he could not kick a very serious GI infection. About three-fourths of the way through the expedition he announced his intention to pack up and head home. But as opposed to that other climber's situation where he was directed to leave the mountain, the guides were desperately trying to talk JR into staying. We all were. He had been a strong climber and a great team player throughout the trip, and no one wanted to see him go home. He was an asset that none of us wanted to lose. I even went as far as to tell him that the Gonzaga Bulldogs were an "okay" basketball team, thinking that might change his mind about leaving. Sadly, he could not be convinced to stay (but he did manage to mumble something about respecting the Duke Blue Devils on his way out of base camp).

In the end, JR didn't summit Everest. But his experience of leaving the mountain was very different than the other man's. He knew he had the respect and affection of his team members. He knew he had their support if he wanted to keep climbing. He knew he was leaving for the right reasons—his own health and safety. That's a successful out-come in my book.

When you treat people well and are kind to them, you

send a signal that you *care*, and people will reciprocate and treat you well as a result. But this book isn't a manual on mountain etiquette. (Although someone should probably write one. *Note to publisher...*) It's about how to have a positive impact on your team. And that's why *caring matters*. If your team knows that you care about them, it helps to build loyalty and trust. Displaying competence is of course very important in the trust-building process as well, but you can be competent and still not have the trust of your team. And in order to achieve maximum results (in whatever you are doing), you need them to trust you.

Don't assume they'll trust you because you have a fancy title or role. For example, don't make the mistake of thinking that because you're a mountain guide people will automatically put their faith in you. "Guide" is just a title. A title might earn trust if you're a guide in Paris and you're giving a tour of the Eiffel Tower or the Louvre. People will trust that you're giving them the correct historical information about these tourist attractions. But titles are meaningless in extreme environments when there is so much on the line.

"Leader" is a mind-set—and that's much more important than a title. I know amateur climbers who have much better leadership skills than some professional guides. Plenty of guides out there just want to climb and collect a paycheck (which they receive regardless of what happens to their team on the mountain), and they provide little or no mentoring or support. These people rarely have anyone's trust.

By contrast, guides who are strong leaders care about helping the team achieve its goals. They help people perform the best they can, and they put the team's interests before their own. And like any good leader, a good guide isn't concerned about getting credit or recognition; he or she is concerned about contributing to the team's overall success. I've learned a lot from accomplished guides who would absolutely put themselves in harm's way to help out people on their team. Those guides are true leaders.

Whether you're leading an expedition or a software development group, your team has to know they are important to you. How do you let them know they matter? One way is to take the time to get to know the people on your team as *individuals*. I don't mean just their names and their hometowns and their favorite foods (chocolate, in case you like this book so much that you are inclined to send me a gift). You should get to know them on a deeper level. Find out about the things that are important to them: their families, their hobbies and interests outside of work, their dreams for the future. This is how strong bonds begin to form. People need to know they matter. Ask questions. It's not hard.

Building trust isn't the only reason to spend time asking people about themselves. The more information you have about someone, the better you can assess their skills and capabilities. You would never buy a car without looking under the hood, no matter how pretty the paint job, right? You want to know how that vehicle is going to perform. Same goes for your climbing partners or anyone who works with you. And the way to learn more is by spending more time talking to them about themselves.

For some people, this seems like common sense. For others, making casual conversation may seem like a waste of energy and time. It's not. Getting to know people as individuals prevents us from drawing erroneous judgments or creating false expectations about what someone can or cannot do. With every layer we peel away, we come upon new tidbits of information that hone our notion of how some-one will likely perform in a demanding situation. The more we know, the better equipped we are to maximize their strengths and help them compensate for their weaknesses (as Eric and George helped me do in Antarctica).

For example, you may have a teammate—let's call him Jake—who appears upon first glance as if he would be a good performer. Tall, fit, and in his early twenties. Off the bat he mentions that he has spent the last year climbing full-time. At first blush, a great sign of dedication and solid experience, someone you would be excited to have on your team. *Perfect!*

But then, after spending some more time asking Jake questions about himself, Jake reveals he is an only child from a wealthy family and has never had an actual job. He had indeed been climbing nonstop for a year, but his par-ents funded all of his trips, and many were private expedi-tions that were organized just for him. He had guides and porters but no other climbers with him—so he has never really had to deal with teammates before. That's a red flag. He may be experienced, but he's also used to getting what he wants, when he wants it.

So knowing all of this, now you have to ask yourself whether Jake is more likely to be a supportive teammate or a high-maintenance personality. Could go either way. I've met plenty of wealthy people who are great teammates. And same with people who don't have siblings. And I've met plenty of people who behave like spoiled brats who don't have money and come from large families. Only way to really know what to expect from this guy is to get to know him better.

Meanwhile, another teammate—Lou—appears to be

in his early sixties, so you might automatically think that there's no way this guy has the strength or ability to get up a big mountain. You might be tempted to discount him simply because he looks older (and he *is* older). But once you engage him in conversation you find out that he's an Ironman triathlete (which shows discipline and stamina), he lives in Washington State close to Mount Rainier, and he has been training there on weekends for a year and a half. You then learn he has climbed six of the Seven Summits and is a self-made businessman. Translation: he's used to hard work and knows what it's like to manage people and be a part of a team. Now your confidence in Lou is bolstered.

Then there is Maria, who has climbed a couple of 8,000-meter peaks and looks pretty fit. She has been climbing longer than anyone else in the group and has decades of experience under her belt. She should be able to tackle the mountain—no problem, right? But what you don't know is that she has never actually made it to the top of any of those peaks and even had to be rescued once during an attempt on a much lower mountain. Hmmmmm. This changes your perspective on how she might handle a long, challenging expedition. She may need more guidance than you antici-pated. The good news is that you've asked the right ques-tions and have uncovered this information, so now you can give her the extra support she may need.

Just as you cannot judge a book by its cover ("But come on—*this book cover is cool!*"), you cannot judge how well a climber will perform by her appearance or even by her climbing résumé. As a leader, you need to take the time to dig deeper. You need to ask the right questions and really get to know people in order to properly assess their abilities. Each individual is going to need a different approach when it comes to helping them perform at their best. The more information you uncover, the more influence you can have as a leader.

Because no two team members are alike, you will need to tailor your coaching style based on the needs of your team. Let's go back to Dennis Rodman again (because we know him already). Yes, he was definitely a handful, more than some coaches were able to manage (his behavior was too erratic and unpredictable). Franchise owners could not get him to conform to team standards. Many of Rodman's own teammates could not figure him out, and they didn't even try to. But Phil Jackson, who was coaching the Chicago Bulls at the time, approached Rodman's issues differently, which made this player-coach relationship extraordinary.

Jackson took the time to dig deeper with Rodman, and based on what he knew about Rodman's difficult upbringing as well as his learning disabilities, he adjusted his expectations. He also adjusted Rodman's training regimen. While the other Bulls players arrived ninety minutes before each game to practice together, Rodman would come just an hour before tip-off and would work out on his own. Why? Because while Rodman was great on the court, he wasn't great at handling stress before a game. Coming early and practicing with the team was a problem for him. He also had attention deficit issues. So rather than forcing Rodman to conform or pressuring him to change his behavior (some of which came from psychological and emotional issues beyond his control), Coach Jackson made adjustments for him. But Rodman wasn't getting off easy. Jackson set up a system where he was fined for not showing up on time (so yeah, he was basically fined for every game). It was a trade-off. The team didn't feel like Rodman was getting away with anything because he always paid for his bad behavior (literally).

Other coaches gave up on Rodman because they saw his behavior as too disruptive. But Jackson dug deeper to learn more about what was going on inside this most unusual player. Instead of simply scolding Rodman for his conduct, Jackson figured out a way to alleviate the things that were hindering him (such as the pregame stress) and showed him love and acceptance. In doing that, he figured out how to harness Rodman's potential. Jackson didn't just care about Dennis the basketball player; he cared about Dennis the person. He knows that loyalty and respect come from showing that you care. And that's why Coach Phil Jackson has the highest percentage of wins (.704) and most titles (eleven championships) of any coach in the NBA. And it's also what makes him a high-impact leader.

So, back to you now. You're asking plenty of questions, you're getting to know the individuals on your team, and you've uncovered lots of helpful information that is going to boost performance—all effective ways to build loyalty and trust, which are touchstones of strong leadership. You're not done. You also need to show your team that you are willing to roll up your sleeves, get your hands dirty, and work side by side with them in order to achieve the common goal. You need to demonstrate that you are willing to take the same risks, endure the same pain, and make the same sacrifices as everyone else.

In other words, your mother lied—*you aren't special.* You may be accomplished, brilliant, and competent, but you aren't special. And you shouldn't act as if you are, because if you want to earn loyalty and trust, your team needs to know that you can relate to them. If they have the impression that you are living in a completely different world than they are and have no idea what it is like to be in their shoes, then your chances of attaining that feeling of unity with your team are slim. But if you show them that you are willing to lock arms with them and work together, you'll earn not only their trust, but also their respect.

In 2010, the CBS network premiered a brilliant new show called *Undercover Boss*, which first debuted in the United Kingdom in 2009. The series, created by Stephen Lambert, won the Primetime Emmy Award for Outstanding Reality Program in 2012. The premise of the show is to fool employees into thinking that they are training a job applicant who is a potential new employee—but unbeknownst to them, the person they are training is actually their company's CEO. The employees think the cameras are there to film a documentary about a particular job within their industry, so they do their best to demonstrate "a day in the life." The CEOs wear disguises, change their names, and come up with a cover so that no one has any idea who they are. Then they spend a week or so rotating through various positions, such as janitorial worker, warehouse team member, forklift operator, or night-shift delivery person—positions that top executives typically don't have a lot of hands-on experience with.

More often than not, the "undercover boss" can barely perform the task he or she is supposed to be learning. And the other employees, who shine through as the real heroes, patiently and diligently work to help this "newbie" master the necessary skills. Throughout this process, the CEO also gets to know each employee he or she is working with on a very personal level. They're together all day, so the conversation runs deep. The employees share their thoughts on their careers or what they think of the company, and often they share ideas they have for improving products and processes. They also talk about their families, their aspirations, their struggles. Because they have no idea they are talking to the CEO, they typically speak very freely and openly.

At the end of the show the CEO's true identity is revealed, and the employees' reactions are always priceless. Most of them practically fall over from shock when they learn that the job applicant is actually the big boss. The employees are typically very moved by the boss's showing of compassion and willingness to listen to their ideas. Many of the employees are rewarded for their loyalty and dedication with promotions or scholarship money or perhaps a donation to a favorite charity. The employees learn that even though they aren't always visible to the senior executives, they are valuable contributors and they have a voice. The CEOs learn what is most important to their people and how they can help one another achieve success—not just in work, but in life.

Chris Carlson is one of three executive producers on the show, and I asked him how they came up with the idea for *Undercover Boss* and what they hoped to accomplish. He explained that the idea came about during the 2008 economic downturn, when many CEOs were portrayed by the media as out-of-touch villains. People believed that while the average American was struggling, CEOs didn't really seem to get it. Carlson told me that they wanted to get America's corporate leaders to "bond with their frontline people in the most basic way—over an honest day's work." That meant getting these CEOs out of their fancy offices and expensive suits and asking them to get out there in the trenches with their employees. The producers of the show hoped that the undercover experience would enable CEOs to garner solid ideas on how they could improve procedures and implement best practices in order to make their company an all-around better place to work.

But the show also revealed some things that the producers didn't expect. "We assumed that we'd see the bosses having a rough time handling the tough work physically," Carlson explained. "But I think what surprised a lot of us was how quickly the show turned into a human drama about perseverance that seemed to demystify and humanize the American CEO."

It's important for leaders to come off as human. But for that to happen, they need to tear down the walls that often exist between them and their employees. Everyone needs to stand together. *Undercover Boss* gave viewers a glimpse of the emotional bonds that form when leaders and their teams do just that.

But you don't have to go undercover on a reality show to bond with your employees and to become an empathetic leader. You can do that on your own. And you should. Take Mark Zuckerberg, for example. The Facebook founder and CEO became the world's youngest billionaire at age twenty-three. He's brilliant. He's a visionary. Clearly, he *is* special. But here's the thing about Zuck—when he is at the office, he doesn't act as if he is special. He doesn't spend his days holed up in some decked-out office up on a penthouse floor, disconnected from the rest of his employees. Rather, he strategically positioned his desk right smack in the middle of the common workspace at Facebook, and he sits with everyone else. In addition, at lunchtime, it isn't unusual to find Zuckerberg waiting in line for Mexican food like everybody else has to do, and then sitting outside on the ground and eating with his employees. Sure, he still spends hundreds of thousands of dollars on private jets, and I'm guessing he isn't staying at too many Howard Johnsons when he's on the road (I have no problem with that—he's earned it), but when he is in the office, he doesn't expect any kind of special treatment. He works right alongside his employees. The message: *we are all in this together.*

In contrast to Zuckerberg's approach, consider John Thain, the former head of the New York Stock Exchange who took over as CEO of Merrill Lynch in 2008. He was forced to step down in 2009, barely a year into the job, amid much controversy, including an unexpected $15 billion loss (yes, that's with a *b*) in the fourth quarter of 2008. But even before the firm's colossal loss, Thain ruffled feathers for spending an inordinate amount of cash on his new office at Merrill—to the tune of $1.2 million, which included the purchase of $90,000 in area rugs, a $1,400 trash can, and a $35,000 toilet (talk about pissing away money...sorry, couldn't resist).

Unlike other infamous CEOs associated with excess, such as Bernie Ebbers (former CEO of WorldCom) and Dennis Kozlowski (former CEO of Tyco), who both went to prison for fraud, Thain wasn't corrupt and didn't break any laws. He was guilty of poor judgment. He was so far removed from the reality that most of his employees faced that people lost faith in his ability to lead. Spending Merrill Lynch's money on the types of things he purchased for his office would be considered excessive even in the best of economic times, but considering the financial crisis that had floored the rest of the country, it was really over the top.

This type of behavior undermines loyalty among employees, because it gives the impression that the leader is out of touch. And clearly John Thain *was* out of touch, which created a backlash rather than feelings of brotherhood. Thain was certainly not the only guilty party among CEOs who lacked a sense of shared values with employees. He just happened to be high profile enough to be a media target.

Your team needs to know that you are willing to endure anything they are asked to endure. They want to know that you are with them, and not just in spirit. In order to build loyalty and trust you should strive to lead like Zuckerberg. I'm not saying you have to go to work in a hoodie and flip-flops every day, but you need to show them that you'll work side by side with them (as Zuckerberg does, *literally*) and that you're there for them when they need you. If you send a message that you are one with your employees, they will feel more loyal and will be motivated to work harder.

Expedition leaders are always right out there in the trenches with their teams. There is no "class" system in these environments. Leaders sleep in the same type of tent as everyone else. They don't stay in luxury accommodations. They are the first ones up in the morning and the last to go to sleep at night. They typically haul more weight in their backpacks than anyone else on the team. They cook the meals and they make sure their teams eat before they down any food themselves, similar to combat troops in the army, where the food order goes in inverse order of rank. Privates, the lowest-ranking soldiers, eat first. The noncommissioned officers (NCOs) don't eat until all of their soldiers are fed. The commissioned officers don't eat until all the NCOs are fed. And after everyone else has had their rations, the commanding officers get their meal.

The "officers eat last" philosophy should apply to all

types of leaders, not just those in the military. Always take care of your people first. If you take care of them, they will take care of you.

File under "Building Loyalty and Trust"

A title does not bring you trust and respect. You have to earn it with your actions. Be good to people. Show your team that you care about them by getting to know them as individuals. Ask lots of questions. Then use the answers to devise more skillful approaches to leading them. Be willing to walk a mile in their shoes (or climb a mile in their boots). The more dedicated you are to your team, the harder they will work for you and for one another.

Chapter 9

IGNORE THE RULES

Do the Right Thing. Always.

Rules usually exist for a reason. But you shouldn't think of them as strict laws that should be followed blindly; instead, rules should be viewed more as guiding principles, as suggestions worth considering versus absolutes. That flexible attitude is essential in dynamic, precarious situations when leaders must make decisions that facilitate the best possible outcomes. Often such decisions require breaking the rules.

Of course if you're going to break the rules, you'd better have a good reason to do so. On March 16, 2006, a group of infantry soldiers, a helicopter crew, and a medical team had a damn good one: a soldier by the name of Channing Moss—and I'll get to his story in a minute.

I first learned of Pvt. Channing Moss from Brig. Gen. (Ret.) Tom Kolditz, who spent twelve years as the head of the Department of Behavioral Sciences and Leadership (BS&L) at the United States Military Academy at West Point.

West Point has been around since 1802; long considered one of the premier leader-development institutions, it's known throughout the world for its commitment to institutional integrity and ethics. Its list of graduates (referred to as the Long Gray Line) includes US presidents, foreign heads of state, astronauts, and decorated military leaders.

As an adjunct professor in General Kolditz's department, I always made a point to sit in on as many of his lectures as I could. He is one of the world's top experts on leading teams in extreme environments and is the author of the book *In Extremis Leadership*, which details various scenarios where individuals voluntarily place themselves in high-risk situations (think military combat leaders, firefighters, FBI hostage negotiators, and so on). These leaders differ from business leaders in that their success is not measured in terms of revenues or market share, but rather in terms of the physical and psychological conditions of their teams and the people they are responsible for. I've gained some invaluable insight from spending time with General Kolditz, and he inspired me to learn more about the art and science of leadership.

In addition to running BS&L, General Kolditz also played an integral part in the design and development of the Thayer Leader Development Group (TLDG), which is an executive education program that shares West Point leadership best practices with leaders from the corporate, nonprofit, and government sectors. I joined TLDG as a board member and strategic advisor shortly after its inception in 2010. In less than four years we have had close to eight thousand executives come through the program to learn about leadership "the West Point Way."

One aspect of leadership cultivation at West Point centers on learning to lead in a VUCA environment. VUCA stands for Volatility, Uncertainty, Complexity, and Ambiguity. VUCA certainly applies to many environments outside of the military, which is why the TLDG program has been so effective and popular with thousands of corporate executives.

The TLDG program content dispels the myth that people in the military are trained to unthinkingly follow the rules. Nothing could be further from the truth. Sound military practice is based on the idea that a VUCA environment will sometimes require improvisation well outside the rules. General Kolditz drove that point home by sharing a video from the Military Times Media Group that told the story of the people who risked their lives to save an injured soldier, Pvt. Channing Moss. Now, it's not easy to wow corporate executives these days. They've seen and heard it all. But the first time I sat in on one of General Kolditz's TLDG sessions, I saw an entire room humbled.

———

Private Moss was unique in that he had been airlifted to Orgun-E Battalion Aid Station on the Afghanistan–Pakistan border…*with an unexploded rocket-propelled grenade (RPG) lodged in his pelvis.* To all parents who freak out when their kid swallows a quarter, or maybe sticks a Cocoa Puff up his nose that he can't get out (a nod to my older brother), let's keep things in perspective going forward.

Here's how it all went down:

Moss was in southeastern Afghanistan riding in a convoy with the 2nd Battalion, 87th Infantry, 3rd Brigade Combat Team, 10th Mountain Division. He had been in Afghanistan for about a month and his platoon was out on its very first patrol, near the Pakistan border. Moss was riding in a Humvee and was manning a Mark 19 machine gun, which fires

40 mm grenades at a rate of sixty rounds per minute with a maximum effective range of 1,500 meters.

The convoy ran into an ambush. They were hit with RPGs and small-arms fire coming from the ridgeline above them. When Moss turned his machine gun to return fire, an RPG— the first of three that would strike his vehicle—exploded against the door. The next two rounds hit the front of the Humvee. One of them obliterated the windshield and sailed past the front passenger seat, slicing through part of Staff Sgt. Eric Wynn's face en route, leaving him badly injured. As Moss positioned himself to return fire, he realized that he smelled something smoldering...which turned out to be *his own flesh*. The unexploded RPG had entered Moss's body and had come to a stop in his thigh, thus turning the young soldier into a human bomb.

Moss later described what was going through his head: "I thought I was never going to get back to my family, I thought I was going to die right there....I thought about my wife and about my girl growing up without me....I thought I was going to die and that they weren't going to be able to save me....I felt at peace at one moment and thought that if I did die, I died for the right cause and I did the right thing...but you want to fight and you want to live."

The company medic, Spec. Jared Angell, one of Moss's best friends, was in the same convoy and immediately came to Moss's aid. He began to bandage his friend's wounds in order to stabilize not only Moss but also the RPG, which had the potential to kill everyone within a thirty-foot radius if it exploded.

Moss's squad radioed for help. Forward Operating Base Salerno dispatched a Black Hawk helicopter carrying a medical team to the scene to evacuate the casualties. Of course there was one critical piece of information the medevac team did not have—the bit about the RPG that was lodged in Moss. His commanding officer was afraid the medevac team wouldn't transport Moss with a live ordnance in him, so he strategically omitted that juicy detail when he called in his report.

Army policy states that soldiers in Moss's condition are not to be transported—which makes perfect sense, as transporting a patient embedded with a live RPG would endanger everyone onboard the helicopter. The proper procedure would be to sandbag him in an area where he would not be a danger to anyone if he exploded, and then give him painkillers and...basically...wait for him to die.

The medevac team that arrived found Moss covered in bandages and blankets. When they lifted the blankets off him to assess his injuries, you can imagine the collective rounds of *"Holy sh*t!"* that came from their mouths. They knew Moss's condition was critical; he was losing blood and was very close to death. But Chief Warrant Officer 3 Jorge Correa, who was piloting the helicopter, wasn't about to give up on Moss. He quickly conferred with the rest of the medevac crew and everyone was in agreement about what they were going to do. *To hell with the rules!* There would be no sandbagging. Even though they knew Moss's chances of survival were slim, they loaded him onto the helicopter and got him the hell out of there, risking all of their lives in the process.

The crew had seen it all during their experience evacuating mortally injured soldiers—limbs blown off, severed heads, you name it—so very little could rattle them at this point. Until now. They were flying the unfriendly skies with a guy who could detonate any second. But according to

Correa, "there was no hesitation" when it came to loading Moss onto that helicopter and transporting him to the battalion aid station where he might have a shot at surviving.

The helicopter touched down at Forward Operating Base Orgun-E. Enter army surgeon Maj. John Oh, a Korean immigrant who became a naturalized US citizen and graduated from West Point. The thirty-six-year-old Oh was barely into his fourth month of deployment with the 10th Mountain Division in Afghanistan when he found himself staring down on the operating table at Channing Moss.

Oh recalls the experience: "After they removed all of his clothing I could clearly see this rod sticking out of his hip, and I was actually looking at it—and I had never seen an RPG before. I realized this looked like some kind of munition because it had fins on it, so it's kind of hard to imagine any other rod that would have fins on it, sticking out of somebody's hip. . . . The guideline is that you're not supposed to bring them into the aid station, you actually leave them outside and treat them as what we call an 'expectant patient,' so you treat him like he is going to blow up, which means you put them outside the aid station, you take precautions to keep them away from the facility. But essentially treat him like an expectant patient, like he's not going to survive. I was scared. I was scared sh*tless, basically. I had never been so scared in my whole life. . . . And then you look at the guy and you think, 'There's no way I am going to let this guy die, it just can't happen. It can't happen.'"

An aid station filled with other patients and medical personnel is no place for a live RPG. That's pretty evident even to those not familiar with army policies. But on that day, for that patient, Major Oh and a medical team chose *not* to go by the rules. As a surgeon, Oh viewed his primary role as saving patients, not allowing them to die. Despite the risks, he decided to ignore the rules in the military's own *Emergency War Surgery* manual. He knew what he had to do.

Oh asked for volunteers who were willing to stay and help with the delicate procedure (many hands went up), and he ordered everyone else out of the operating room; obviously, he didn't want to risk more lives than necessary. He called in the Explosive Ordnance Disposal (EOD) team, and they all went to work on what would be the most frightening procedure any of them had ever performed. "At that point I don't think anyone thought about the dangers to themselves. We just thought about getting this thing out as fast as possible.... This thought went through my head that these were the last people I was ever going to see, potentially."

Oh looked at them all and said, "If this thing goes off, I just want you all to know it's been great working with you."

Sgt. First Class Dan Brown, the EOD tech who had been called in, explained the situation to everyone in the room to make sure they understood the risks of the procedure. "Worst-case scenario, we could bring the roof down on top of us...but you would already be dead by the time the roof hit the ground." Okay then...

They began cutting open Channing Moss's abdomen to assess the damage to his organs and to get a better look at the RPG that was lodged inside him. He had lost a lot of blood and had extensive intestinal damage and a shattered pelvis, but no other life-threatening injuries (besides the obvious). At one point Moss's heart stopped as a result of the blood loss. Chest compressions were not an option, so they injected him with epinephrine, which did the trick. His heart was beating again. So far the score was Channing Moss: 2, Death: 0. But there was still a lot of painstaking work to do. Intricate, delicate, lifesaving, life-risking work. And all of it against army rules.

The good news was that Sergeant Brown could tell that the most dangerous part of the RPG—the portion that was capable of setting off the largest explosion—was in fact *not* inside their patient. Of course what was still there had enough *oomph* to kill Channing Moss and take off a few other people's limbs as well. He began sawing the tail fin off the RPG with a hacksaw. Once the fin was removed, they pulled the explosive device out of Moss's devastated body and got it *the hell out* of the aid station, then off to a location where they could detonate it safely. Moss was alive. So were the rest of the medical personnel. And everyone still had their limbs attached.

Sergeant Brown recalled how it felt to be a critical part of the lifesaving surgery that day: "It was a feeling of tension, of course, but of amazement at the same time that we were able to be involved in doing something like this and removing an RPG from a person that was still alive. Our whole thought the entire time was how to keep Channing Moss alive....I was inside myself. I was doing what I was doing and had no distractions until the moment the RPG was out of my hands, and that's when the world came back into play....I just sat down and started shaking....It was complete release. Just complete amazement and release at the same time. And, 'oh my God, we just finished something that saved a kid's life.'"

Not a lot of people would have had the brass to do what Major Oh and the rest of his team did that day—they broke protocol and took action to save a life while risking theirs. Their heroism is a truly extreme example of bypassing the traditional rules in an unusually extreme situation. Oh explained his rationale: "I did it because I knew that he had a chance to make it, but the basic reason was that Channing Moss was looking at me and talking and breathing, that's why I did it." Even after the fact, Oh gets choked up when he recalls what his team was able to do that day. "For me to do it once, when he [Moss] shows up, I don't think that's a very heroic thing. For these guys to go outside the wire and put themselves at risk every day, *that's heroic*." Humility: another important leadership trait.

Channing Moss knows he owes his life to a lot of people—from his commanding officers to the people who were with him when his Humvee was hit, the flight crew, the surgical team, the bomb techs, and so on. He doesn't hesitate to express his gratitude. "All those people that volunteered to do what they had to do, they could have died at any time, and they could have blown up and they could be missing arms and legs right now because I still had a live ordnance in me.... They took the initiative. Thank God.... Thank God for those people, being in the position they were in at the time. I owe them my life." Three months after the attack, Moss's second daughter, Ariana, was born. And he was right there in the delivery room with his wife, Lorena.

Those who played a significant role in Saving Private Moss were recognized by the army.

Staff Sgt. Eric Wynn, whose face was sliced open when the rocket-propelled grenade came through their Humvee but who still managed to radio for help, received the Purple Heart, which is awarded to members of the Armed Forces who are killed or wounded in action against an enemy of the United States.

Spec. Jared "Doc" Angell, the medic who first attended to Moss in the field when the injury occurred, was awarded the Bronze Star with Valor for his act of heroism.

Sgt. First Class Dan Brown from the EOD team was also awarded the Bronze Star with Valor. He was later promoted to master sergeant and went on to serve in Saudi Arabia as an EOD advisor to the Saudi military.

The medevac team that transported Moss—Chief Warrant Officer 3 Jorge Correa (pilot), Sgt. John Collier (flight medic), Chief Warrant Officer 3 Jeremy Smith (copilot), and Staff Sgt. Christian Roberts (crew chief)—were awarded the Air Medal for heroism during aerial flight.

Maj. Kevin Kirk (now a lieutenant colonel), an orthopedic surgeon who also operated on Moss, received an Army Commendation Medal with Valor. He is the chief of foot and ankle surgery at Brooke Army Medical Center in Texas.

Maj. John Oh received the Soldier's Medal, which is given for a heroic act not involving actual conflict with an armed enemy. You don't receive that award for just saving a life—you have to have performed an act that involved personal hazard or danger and the voluntary risk of life. No doubt Oh's actions qualified. He published an account of the surgical procedure in the textbook *War Surgery in Afghanistan and Iraq*, which somehow didn't make Amazon's list of best books of the year, but I'm still going to recommend it to my book club. Dr. Oh was promoted to lieutenant colonel in 2009. He is currently working at Landstuhl Regional Medical Center in Germany, which in 2011 became the first Level 1 trauma center located outside of the United States. Oh is the trauma program director there. I can't imagine there is a better man for the job.

And what became of Channing Moss? Well, he earned a

Purple Heart and was able to stand on his own to receive it. He is currently living in Georgia with his wife and is raising two daughters. After years of arduous physical therapy, Moss is able to walk with the aid of only a cane. No more wheelchair or metal walker. The staff at Walter Reed Army Medical Center refers to him as "Rocket Man."

So, back to the topic of rules. We know great things can happen when you break the rules. Likewise, great damage can be done when you robotically follow rules. The Long Island Power Authority learned that that hard way in 2011, when they were unwilling to bend on a long-standing rule and billed a community for using their utility poles during a parade honoring a local hero, 1st Lt. Joseph Theinert.

Theinert, a member of the Army National Guard who had volunteered for active duty, was killed in Kandahar, Afghanistan, in June 2010. He was twenty-four years old. Theinert was in the process of disabling an improvised explosive device (IED) when he realized it was going to explode. He was able to warn the other members of his platoon before the explosion that killed him, and that warning saved twenty lives.

About a year after his death, the men who served with Theinert planned to make a trip to his hometown to pay homage to the brave soldier who had saved their lives. Theinert was from Shelter Island, New York, a Long Island community that has a total area of just over twelve square miles of land and less than three thousand year-round residents (the population can triple in the summers). In other words, it's a very tight community.

To honor their fallen comrade, Theinert's fellow soldiers made the eight-hour, four-hundred-mile trip from Fort Drum, which is in northwest New York State. The Theinert family was initially expecting twenty soldiers to come, but the number grew to more than forty. Clearly there were a lot of people who wanted to make the journey to Shelter Island in honor of Theinert.

Boy did Shelter Island roll out the red carpet for these soldiers! A huge parade was planned. The fire department, the American Legion color guard, and other service members of the local community were all going to be there to welcome these men to Shelter Island. The group even had travel escorts the entire way, ranging from law enforcement to organized motorcycle groups that honor our fallen heroes, including the Patriot Guard Riders and the Red Knights.

The town was appropriately "dressed" for the occasion. The American Legion even purchased brand-new, heavy-duty American flags from Shelter Island Hardware and hung them on the utility poles along the main parade route. The flags would remain up from Memorial Day through the Fourth of July as a tribute to Theinert and to all war veterans. The local papers, of course, carried the story of this gathering of the entire community to honor one of their own.

The Long Island Power Authority (LIPA)—the local utility company—got wind of the parade plans and did something kind of hard to comprehend. LIPA billed the town of Shelter Island for hanging the flags on its poles. Apparently, no one in the community realized there was a fee associated with hanging the flags on the poles—$1.25 for each pole, to be exact. (It is normally $5 per pole, but LIPA was kind enough to prorate the amount, since the town planned to display the flags for only two months. I'm not sure how LIPA worked out the math for that—you'd have to ask them.) The grand total was a mere $23, but of course it wasn't the money that angered the Shelter Island residents, it was the fact that

LIPA would send them any kind of bill for hanging American flags on their poles! It was about the principle, not about the money.

Now, you would *think* that someone within LIPA would have simply waived the fee. But no one did, because apparently charging a fee to use the poles was "the rule." Of course the rule was not put into place with American flags in mind, but rather for situations where other companies wanted to hang wire for cable or phone lines. No one at LIPA apparently thought this through; they simply said, "But those are the rules." Well, that $23 bill was responsible for generating a massive amount of ill will toward LIPA. When the story hit the national media, LIPA had a serious PR problem.

LIPA tried to do damage control. A company spokesperson came forward to explain that LIPA management agreed that the rule shouldn't apply in this situation. But they also claimed they had no choice but to send out the bill, because state law required it and they did not have the authority to waive it. This doesn't wash. But while LIPA may not have had the authority to waive the fee, it seems as if there were better ways to handle the situation.

The most obvious option would have been for LIPA to pay the $23 itself. I'm guessing that most of their executives wouldn't have missed the twenty-three bucks had one of them shelled it out personally. And if the bill somehow was sent without anyone taking notice, as things do occasionally slip through the cracks, they could have responded differently. Instead of saying, "Hey, this isn't our fault, we have to follow the rules," they could have said something to the effect of, "We regret that the bill was sent out—it shouldn't have been. It was an administrative error on our part. We are grateful to all veterans for their selfless service and are making a donation of $10,000 to [*insert chosen veteran's charity here*] in honor of Lt. Theinert." That would have done the trick. People are surprisingly more forgiving when companies (and people) take responsibility for mistakes.

LIPA's chief operations officer did end up covering the bill himself—but too late to repair the damage to the firm's reputation, especially in the community of Shelter Island.

And, oh, I forgot to mention: Verizon owned the majority of the poles on which the community hung the flags along the parade route, and they waived their fee without a second thought. Part of Verizon's company credo is, "We voice our opinion and exercise constructive dissent, and then rally around the agreed-upon action with our full support."

I would say that LIPA could have benefitted from some constructive dissent in this situation. Leaders who simply follow rules never become skilled at how to handle situations that take them off course from their plans. And playing outside the rules is often your only choice in dynamic environments, where there is often no set of rules in place about how to react when unforeseen circumstances hit.

In the mountains, as in business or any other part of your life, you have to deal with factors that you have absolutely zero control over. Weather is only one great example. Sometimes you look up at a mountain's summit, and from a distance it looks like it might be fairly approachable—calm winds, blue skies. But within a matter of minutes, a storm can blow in. Suddenly your summit dreams are in tatters, and you're wondering if you can even make it safely down to your tent (which could also be in tatters).

The key to surviving storms is the *ability to take action based on the situation at the time*, regardless of the plan. Because whatever plan you came up with last year, last month, last week—*or even this morning*—it is already out-dated. Plans are outdated as soon as they are finished in environments that change very rapidly. That's why leaders who are hell-bent on sticking to the rules or sticking to their plans or sticking to the way things have always been done in the past are headed for failure.

The following year came a much bigger challenge. The mother of all VUCA environments—Hurricane Sandy. This time the fallout for LIPA would be much worse than just a few nasty news stories.

Hurricane Sandy didn't appear out of nowhere. While storm forecasts are often inaccurate, this time the National Hurricane Center (NHC) pretty much nailed it as far as where and when she would hit land and how much of a punch she would pack. Not only were the forecasts accurate with regard to the location and intensity of the storm, but the NHC also got the information out *five days prior* to the storm hitting. That warning gave people on the East Coast time to prepare for the storm's impact and thus saved hundreds, if not thousands, of lives.

Yet despite that heads-up, LIPA's leadership failed to prepare for Sandy. The board of trustees held a meeting four days before the storm of the century was due to hit. According to the *New York Times*, they skimmed over the subject before moving on to other topics—one of which was hiring branding consultants. Sandy clobbered the East Coast on October 29, 2012, knocking out power for 90 percent of LIPA's 1.1 million customers; some forty thousand customers still had no power more than two weeks after the storm. And while sometimes it's tough to predict what will happen when natural disasters strike, LIPA had plenty of data points. A year or so earlier, Hurricane Irene had left half a million of their customers without power for nine days, so it's not like LIPA had no experience with big storms.

The firm's antiquated monitoring and information systems were part of the problem. LIPA had not spent the millions of dollars required to upgrade their systems, even though Irene had underscored their need to do just that. Imagine if the authorities in the San Francisco Bay Area had reacted that way to the 1989 Loma Prieta earthquake (magnitude 6.9): "Sorry, we aren't going to do the seismic retrofit on our buildings and bridges." In addition to its shortsighted failures pre–Hurricane Sandy, LIPA also lacked the proper systems to communicate with customers *after* the storm. Many customers didn't have a clue about when they could expect power to return. Calls to LIPA's call centers went unanswered. Customers were routinely promised that LIPA service crews would come to help them...but all too often, no one showed up.

There's no worse leadership failure following a disastrous event than a combination of a lack of communication and broken promises. The raging criticism leveled at LIPA in the aftermath of Sandy ultimately resulted in the resignations of a number of LIPA's top executives. With luck, a new generation of leaders will learn from their predecessors' experiences.

LIPA has made some serious missteps over the years. The situation with the American flags was related to an inability (or unwillingness) to break the rules. The issues with Hurricane Sandy reflected a deeper and closely related problem: a lack of guiding principles. Companies often cling blindly to rules (or short-term goals like maximizing quarterly profits or meeting a certain deadline) even when it undermines the true mission. That's why every firm needs to have guiding principles in place to influence their employees' behaviors and actions (more on this theme in the next chapter). This helps ensure they will make smart choices in those instances where the rules should be tossed or when different goals are in conflict. In this case, the guiding principle both before and after the storm should have been: "Take care of your customers, even if it means trimming short-term profits."

When you have these guiding principles in place, people will have a much easier time knowing what constitutes doing the right thing. In the business world where competition is cutthroat, I see countless examples of employees who blindly follow rules at the expense of their customer relationships. I can't tell you how many times while traveling I have asked for a slightly later check-out at my hotel, only to be told by a front desk clerk that in order to keep my room past noon I would need to talk to a manager, and "So sorry, ma'am, there is no manager here now, so you cannot check out at one thirty p.m." *Really?*

This would not happen at the Ritz-Carlton, where hotel employees are empowered to make decisions on their own and are given a $2,000 budget to use at their discretion to "get customer service right" for guests. When the economy is in the tank and every dollar spent at your hotel matters, why would you not just tell the nice, exhausted lady from room 501 that of course she can stay in her room an extra hour and a half? Instead, you have given her an anecdote about your hotel's crappy customer service to share with her friends and publish in her book.

Leaders need to make sure that the people on their teams know when to follow the rules and when to interpret them in ways that lead to better outcomes. Obviously not all outcomes are a matter of life or death, or of preventing PR disasters. Everyday rules can also be ignored if doing so means achieving more favorable results.

File under "Breaking the Rules"

Whether it's someone's health or a paying customer's business that is on the line, there are always situations where you need to break the rules. Rigidity is just as dangerous as complacency. If leaders are in the habit of saying, "These are the rules, and we can't change them," progress will never be made—and worse, irreparable damage can be done. Break the rules. Bust 'em to high hell. Use your judgment and do the right thing. It's as simple as that.

Chapter 10

YOUR THREE WORDS

What's Your Mantra?

CEOs can't be everywhere at once (unless they have spy-cams in everyone's cubicles, but most have better things to do than monitor their staff's every move). Leaders have to trust their people to do the right thing even when they aren't being watched. If a company has a set of guiding principles that represent the heart of its organization, and its employees follow these principles, then their making tough decisions and using good judgment in ambiguous situations becomes much easier. This is why companies need to have credos.

Some of the business leaders who are involved with the Fuqua/Coach K Center on Leadership and Ethics have shared their thoughts about company credos at our board meetings. I hear over and over how important they are and why every employee must understand why the company credo exists and what it really means. That's another way of saying that employees need to know what they are working toward when they go to work every day.

Bill Weldon, who retired as CEO of Johnson & Johnson in 2012, explained how J&J—a very decentralized organization with 250 operating companies and more than 125,000 employees—maintains alignment of purpose through their credo. J&J's credo is a full page in length and details its responsibilities to health-care providers, patients, employees, and the community. It covers everything from providing quality products and reducing costs, to encouraging open communication and continuing innovation. Weldon explained, "The credo is our bull's-eye—the heart and soul of the company. It's not just delivering results…but *how* you deliver them that is important."

Our board has also frequently discussed the fragility of reputations and the fact that a person or company can spend years building a reputation and then lose it in a single day. For example, Billy Campbell, who is CEO of Forbes Travel Guide and was formerly the president of Discovery Networks, talked about signing a major sponsorship deal with Lance Armstrong. He noted that up until October 2012, he would have said that signing Lance was his proudest moment. Now, not so much. The cyclist is banned for life from competing in the sport that made him an icon. His name will be forever associated with the doping scandal that ruined his career.

Joe Bailey, who formerly served both as the CEO of the Miami Dolphins and as vice president of administration of the Dallas Cowboys, brought up the subject of bounties in pro football (financial incentives for players to deliberately injure opponents in order to knock them out of the game). Joe nailed it when he said that integrity should always be at the heart of your enterprise. "You are a brand. And everything that can happen to you can hurt your brand, so you need to protect it." Joe's feeling was that bounties would never be considered, under any circumstances, if the team leadership was truly focused on creating a culture of integrity. "You can put prevention systems in place to stop this from happening, but if you have a culture of integrity it will dissuade people from taking part in any of these kinds of things [bounties]. It's all about protecting your brand."

Penn State learned all this the hard way. Beloved football coach Joe Paterno was a great source of university pride for decades—until former assistant coach Jerry Sandusky was indicted on fifty-two counts of child sexual abuse (and found guilty of forty-five). The university found out that Paterno had done far too little to follow up on early reports of Sandusky's behavior. Some go as far as to say he turned a blind eye. Coach Paterno was fired. He died several months later of cancer and, I am guessing, a broken heart.

Look at Michael Vick, a Heisman Trophy contender in college and the overall first pick in the 2001 NFL draft. He led the Atlanta Falcons to the playoffs twice. But the gridiron clearly didn't provide Vick with the type of competition he craved, because off the field he became involved in an illegal dog-fighting ring, then ended up in prison.

End of story? Nope. Vick got out of prison after almost two years and signed with the Philadelphia Eagles. He was named Comeback Player of the Year in 2010. And while Vick lost his $2 million endorsement deal with Nike in 2007 (felony convictions will do that), he was re-signed by them again in 2011.

He may be a great player, but my 110-pound black Lab and I won't cheer for the Eagles. I don't care if Vick has set a record for most yards rushed by a quarterback. I will always think of him as the guy who got his kicks by torturing and killing dogs. "Don't people deserve a second chance?" you ask. Sure. I realize that Vick paid his dues by serving time, and I *do* think everyone deserves a shot at redemption. Hell, who doesn't love a comeback story? And maybe Vick *has* changed. But I think that the endorsement deal with Nike sends a bad message: talent trumps ethics. The sad truth is that we are quick to overlook character flaws when people perform really well.

My hat is off to Atlanta Falcons owner Arthur Blank, who didn't want Vick back on his team after the dog-fighting scandal. Blank knew Vick was a talented quarterback, and he'd made it clear that he believed Vick deserved a second chance in the NFL, but he wasn't willing to put Vick back in a Falcons uniform.

"Win at any cost" is a credo, but it's a bad one. It's not the way to go. I'm not even sure it leads to more victories in the long run, and it's no way to live. Unfortunately, many in the world of competitive sports seem to have that mindset. I think that all sports teams should have credos that everyone lives and breathes in order to work toward that culture of integrity that Joe Bailey talked about. Then when they hear that an assistant coach is abusing children, they will know exactly what to do—regardless of whether the resulting publicity will "hurt the program."

Individuals should also have credos. We all need a set of key words that remind us of how we want to behave in our professional and personal lives. Those words can provide a lens through which we see and engage the world—not just when we are up against the ropes, but 24/7. West Point's credo consists of three words that influence cadets' lives long after they have left the United States Military Academy. These words are: Duty. Honor. Country.

On May 12, 1962, Gen. Douglas MacArthur gave a speech to West Point cadets and gave meaning to those words: "Those three hallowed words reverently dictate what you ought to be, what you can be, what you will be. They are your rallying point to build courage when courage seems to fail, to regain faith when there seems to be little cause for faith, to create hope when hope becomes forlorn."

The current mission statement of West Point reads as follows: "To educate, train, and inspire the Corps of Cadets so that each graduate is a commissioned leader of character committed to the values of Duty, Honor, Country and prepared for a career of professional excellence and service to the nation as an officer in the United States Army."

Note that the mission statement also mentions a "*career* of selfless service to the nation." The commitment to Duty, Honor, and Country doesn't end when graduates leave West Point, nor does it end when or if they leave the military. These words are meant to stay with them for life; no matter where they are or what they are doing.

A personal credo can help you stay true to yourself and to your beliefs even in extreme circumstances, when risks to your physical and mental well-being might threaten your values. What's your credo? What is your purpose? What do you strive to do daily? How do you think people would currently describe you as a person? As a leader? How do you *want* people to describe you? What values are most important to you? *Know what you stand for.* And know what you would fight for. How do you want to be remembered when you leave this earth?

Here's another question to ask yourself: *What are you are doing right now* to work toward that personal credo? A credo isn't about writing a few words down. It's about taking action. It's about living those words every day.

Coming up with a credo can be a superinteresting process. It requires you to look deep inside. You have to investigate your values and articulate them in a form that inspires you. You don't have to have something as detailed and lengthy as Johnson & Johnson's credo. You can even narrow it down to a phrase or just a few words—call it a *mantra*. (Note to wise guys: we're looking for something a little deeper than "Mmm Mmm Good.") Your mantra might change over the years as your values evolve or as new words or phrases arise, and that's okay, too (which is why it's best not to tattoo it anywhere on your body). Maybe you need a few sentences—fine—but come up with something that represents both who you are and who you want to become.

So, what's *my* mantra? *"Count on me."* I aspire to be the clutch player—the person who others can always count on. I want to be the go-to person when my loved ones or colleagues or teammates need help. I want others to think of me as the person who always follows through on a commitment. I will never let you down when I tell you I am going to give you my all.

A credo, or mantra (call it what you like), offers a ready-made platform for the kind of leadership you want to embody in your life as well. Making a conscious effort to demonstrate your credo will help build your identity as a leader. I've noticed over the years that if you live by your mantra, it's easier to gain the trust and loyalty of the people on your team, because they know what to expect from you. Here's an example:

After spending a few years studying the art and science of leadership, I began lecturing at various meetings and conferences. I developed material that presented leadership lessons in a context much different from that used by most leadership experts. I wanted a platform that would enable me to share this information with various corporate entities, associations, and government organizations.

I had been trying for months to get some of the major speakers bureaus around the country to consider representing me. These bureaus represented famous politicians, professional sports coaches, military heroes, business leaders, authors, entrepreneurs, and the like. None of them would give me the time of day. I would cold-call them and say things like, "I am going to be in your area next week for some meetings, and I am wondering if it might be possible to pop into your office for ten minutes and introduce myself." No one wanted to see me. They would reply with some kind of dismissal like, "Well, we only meet with speakers who are on our roster," which made no sense to me. If they refused to meet with me, then how was I supposed to get on their roster? In fact, how was *anyone* supposed to get on their roster? It was kind of funny (in an incredibly frustrating way).

I kept cold-calling bureaus and continued to pitch myself as a keynote speaker on the topic of leadership. The responses I got usually went something like:

"We already have quite a few leadership speakers and CEOs on our roster. Have you ever run a Fortune 500 company?"

"Well, no," I would say. "But I have run other things… like errands."

Click.

Then I tried the adventure speaker angle. I would tell them I had climbed peaks all over the world and had completed grueling polar expeditions in the most extreme environments known to man. To that I would get reactions like, "Hmmm...have you lost any body parts? Maybe cut off an arm or something?"

That last was obviously a reference to Aron Ralston, the adventurer who was trapped by a boulder in a Utah canyon and cut off his own arm. Aron is the subject of the Oscar-nominated movie *127 Hours*. He was killing it on the speaking circuit. And rightly so—his story of survival is pretty incredible.

Sure, I had endured a couple of cardiac procedures, but when your surgery is performed by a licensed surgeon with sterile instruments in a hospital versus doing it yourself with an old, dull pocketknife in Canyonlands National Park, it doesn't really have the same "wow factor." In short, none of the bureaus had much of an interest in talking to me, let alone booking me as a conference speaker. I eventually realized that if you aren't an Olympic athlete or a CEO or the subject of an Oscar-nominated movie or a best-selling author or *someone* with *some* kind of name-recognition, the bureaus generally aren't interested.

One bureau took pity on me and did let me come in for a chat. Keppler Speakers is located in the Washington, DC, area—not exactly in my backyard, since I was living in California at the time. I called them and told them the same fib I had told every other bureau: "I am going to be in your area next week, could I please pop in and say hello?" And to my surprise, they said, "Sure. We always like to meet new speakers."

I was *in*! Well...it was progress anyway. I didn't know if

Keppler would seriously consider adding me to their roster, but I did know that I could at least set foot in their offices without someone calling security.

I immediately started thinking about what I could do to stand out from the other athletes and industry experts who were also knocking on Keppler's door. What could I do to show them that they should be working with me? How could I demonstrate my personal credo? How could I show them that they could always count on me to give my all?

With those questions in mind, I spent some time on the Keppler website. I looked at the photos of the people who worked there and memorized everyone's names so that when I met them in person, I could greet them before they introduced themselves. I also studied the brief bios that included people's interests and hobbies. I memorized random facts about each member of the Keppler team so when they walked into the conference room for our meeting I could offer up something like, "Ah, you're Eliot Gunner—the horse-racing fan!" I knew who liked baseball and who liked gardening and who was a Carolina basketball fan (I was still gracious to that guy, by the way). They would either consider me to be well-prepared…or a stalker. My hope was that when I left their office in Arlington, Virginia, they would know that they could always count on me to go above and beyond the call of duty.

I figured my depth of preparation would show them that this meeting was important to me and that they, as individuals, were also important to me. Once they all sat down around the large oval conference room table I gave them a brief overview of my speech topic, which was leadership lessons learned from my various mountaineering and polar expeditions. Jim Keppler, who founded the bureau back in

1983, said to me, "Thank you so much for coming in. I think we can do some business with you." *Yessssssss!* I was absolutely thrilled.

Did I hear from them after that? *No!* Well, at least not right away. Radio silence after the meeting.

Six months went by...and then I got a call. It came from one of their most senior agents, Gary McManis. I think it was a Wednesday evening—maybe 6:30 Gary's time. "Alison? Gary McManis from Keppler Speakers here. I have an opportunity that I think might be a good fit for you. What are the chances that you could get yourself to Vegas before tomorrow morning at seven a.m.?"

I was intrigued. They had a client who was in a bind. Jeff Hurt was the conference planner for a large association that was holding a meeting for six thousand people at Mandalay Bay Hotel and Casino. Hurt had a star-studded lineup of keynote speakers. That afternoon the attendees had been treated to an hour with Major League Baseball Hall-of-Famer Cal Ripken Jr. The next morning Carolyn Kepcher, Donald Trump's associate from *The Apprentice*, was scheduled to do the opening keynote. This was back in 2006, when *The Apprentice* was a top-rated show. Carolyn was not only a big television personality at the time, but she was also a successful businesswoman and served as the executive vice president, chief operating officer, and general manager for the Trump National Golf Club.

Unfortunately, Carolyn was sick. She wasn't going to be able to show up for the conference to deliver her scheduled presentation on business lessons she learned from *The Apprentice*. Now, when it's an internal company meeting and the speaker is a no-show, you can just tell all the employees that they will have an extra hour of free time and they'll happily check voice mail and e-mail and kill the sixty minutes. But when it is an association meeting, and the participants have paid to attend the conference, and perhaps some decided to attend solely based on hearing a particular speaker—well, you've got a problem.

I told Gary I could make the 10:30 p.m. flight and would land in Vegas around midnight, plenty of time to make the 8:00 a.m. opening keynote. The sound check was at 7:00 a.m., so that left me seven hours to come up with my material (six if I wanted to take a shower and iron my suit). Gary gave me Jeff Hurt's phone number so that I could call and introduce myself before I got there, since he had absolutely no idea who the hell I was or what I was going to talk about when I stood up in front of those conference attendees.

I called Jeff and told him a little bit about my background and about my various climbs, including the first American Women's Everest Expedition. I then asked him the one most important question I needed an answer to in order for me to prepare an impactful presentation for his conference: "What message do you want the audience to walk away with after my keynote?" And Jeff answered, "Message? I don't care what message you deliver, I just want to make sure that my audience isn't furious about the fact that Carolyn Kepcher isn't here."

Of course there was absolutely nothing Carolyn could have done to get to the conference—when you're hugging a toilet, you can't get on a plane. But her untimely illness ended up giving me the idea for the messaging I would build my speech around that day. So for that—I thank her.

My challenge had been spelled out for me. I knew what I had to do. When I finally arrived at Mandalay Bay, Jeff Hurt was waiting out in front to meet me. I hopped out of the town car and he approached me and introduced himself. "Awwww, you didn't have to wait up for me to arrive," I told him.

"Uh, yes, I did!" he explained. "I just had a celebrity speaker cancel on me at the last minute. I wanted to make sure the replacement actually got here."

Understandable. "I'm here. And don't worry. I will make sure your audience is happy tomorrow morning."

I wasn't yet sure how I was going to make that happen. I figured spiking their coffee would be the best way, but I was fairly certain I couldn't get the Mandalay Bay Convention Center's catering staff on board with that. My other option was to head straight to my hotel room and spend the next five hours putting together a program that would surprise both the audience and my new best friend, Jeff Hurt. I was so grateful that he was giving me the opportunity to address his conference attendees. But the reality was that he had little choice. He had called every major speakers bureau in the country trying to get a celebrity replacement for Carolyn, and none of them could get him anyone on such short notice. Keppler Speakers was the bureau that had come up with someone, and that someone was me. I had no name recognition, which meant I was even more of a gamble for Jeff, who had no idea what to expect from me. He didn't know my story (hell, I hadn't even written my speech yet) and wasn't familiar with my platform style (neither was I). As a conference planner, his reputation was on the line.

So I went to work. I sat alone in that hotel room, trying to figure out what I was going to do to win over the audience. All I knew was that six thousand people were expecting to hear Carolyn Kepcher in the morning, and it was up to me to deliver a presentation that would ensure they weren't disappointed by her absence. I came up with what I thought was a pretty good plan and stayed up through dawn working on my slides. I did not get one single minute of sleep. I couldn't. I had too much work to do, because I had committed to delivering—not a speech, but delivering on a promise to make sure the audience was satisfied with the program. I wanted to deliver on my mantra: Count on me.

Little did I know that this one presentation would alter the course of my career.

At 7:00 a.m., I made my way downstairs for the sound check and to load the slide deck I'd been up all night creating. All was in order. At 8:00 a.m. I walked out onto the stage and greeted the thousands of people who were expecting a tall, leggy blonde. First thing I did was break it to them that Carolyn had canceled at the last minute because she was sick, so they were now getting a short brunette. That was obvious, of course. No one threw rotten tomatoes (or if they did, none of them managed to hit the stage). I breathed a small sigh of relief.

Next thing I did was bring up a slide of Carolyn Kepcher's photo along with her speech title, "Business Lessons Learned from *The Apprentice*." Then I used animation to cross out Carolyn's name, and I had "YOU'RE FIRED" (a phrase famously used at the end of each episode of her TV show) appear across the screen. I jokingly announced that Carolyn had just been "fired." Then I showed her title slide changing from "Business Lessons Learned from *The Apprentice*" to "Business Lessons Learned from *Climbing Mt. Everest*." Now the audience had a glimpse of what was coming.

I had Photoshopped pictures of Carolyn and Donald Trump into my slides, which showed the two of them climbing various mountains. I wanted to build them into my presentation, since the audience was expecting material that had something to do with *The Apprentice*. The main theme of my keynote: *Be the person who always comes through.* Be the person whom everyone can count on when times are most challenging. I even showed a photo of me with a huge grin on my face that was taken just after I had vomited all over myself at 24,000 feet on Mount Everest—and I talked about how, as a leader, you have to push through the toughest of times and show up with a good attitude and be there for your team. I said something to the effect of, "Even when you feel like puking you have to put a smile on your face and get out there and do your job, because it's not about you—it's about the people around you to whom you are accountable. So you need to keep pushing forward. Even when it hurts." The audience reacted with cheers and applause. I spoke for an hour about leadership, teamwork, and how to adapt to a changing environment. Most of all, I talked about the importance of coming through for people when they are counting on you, no matter how difficult or painful or uncomfortable the situation might be.

At the end of my talk I got a rousing standing ovation. Not bad for my first big speech! But, man, what a way to cut my teeth as a keynote speaker. Jeff Hurt came rushing backstage to meet me after my speech and said, "Okay, you just knocked it out of the park. But I saw you arrive at one a.m., so *how did you put that presentation together?*"

I explained to him I had stayed up throughout the morning hours creating the slides and had yet to go to sleep.

He expressed his appreciation and said, "I can't believe you would do that. I don't know many people who would go to the lengths you did for this audience."

"Of course I would do that," I said. "Why would you expect anything less?"

He smiled and said, *"Why have I never heard of you?* No offense, but I must tell you that I had never heard your name before yesterday. None of the bureaus have ever mentioned you to me when I have been exploring options for speakers in the past." Jeff had booked hundreds of speakers and wondered how it was possible that I wasn't on his radar.

I explained my situation to him. *"Confession.* I cannot get the bureaus to talk to me. I have been trying for a year to get in the door with many of them, and very few will give me the time of day. I cannot even get these people to return my phone calls."

Jeff said, "I work with every major speakers bureau in the country, and I am going to contact all of them and let them know what you did here this morning."

At the end of the multiday program at Mandalay Bay, the attendees filled out evaluations. I somehow ended up as the highest-rated speaker at the conference. Jeff shared the survey results with me, and I was really pleased with the positive feedback from the audience. There was, however, *one* comment from an attendee that was not positive: "We should have been told about the replacement. It is obvious that Carolyn canceled a while ago. Alison's presentation was not put together overnight. Communication is very important, and I am disappointed [the association] does not think the same."

Whoever wrote that remark had meant it as a criticism of the association that sponsored the meeting, but I took it as the ultimate compliment.

Of course I could have just used a generic slide presentation that day instead of crafting something completely new, but it wouldn't have had the impact that the customized presentation did. I wanted the audience to walk out of there with the feeling that there was nowhere else they would rather have been than in that room. I wanted to come through for my new team, which included Keppler Speakers, Jeff Hurt, and the six thousand other people who were in the room with me that morning. That's the power of personal credo.

Just as I had come through for Jeff, he came through for me. He called all the major speakers bureaus around the country, and within one week agents were ringing my phone off the hook and asking me to send them my materials. Things took off from there.

My topics have transitioned over the years as I garnered additional leadership lessons from new expeditions. But regardless of the audience I am addressing, the message about the importance of always coming through for your team—even when you feel like puking—is always in there somewhere. I am now exclusively represented by a fabulous speakers bureau and address close to one hundred audiences a year.

Which bureau? Keppler Speakers, of course—the one bureau that was willing to give me a shot when no one else would.

If you are leading teams in extreme environments—because there is so much uncertainty involved—you must have the trust and loyalty of the people on your team. Follow through on your commitments, come hell or high water (or high altitude). People have to know that you will go to the mat for them. That builds trust and gives people confidence in your ability to lead. I strive to always be the person who comes through no matter what, on and off the mountain. And I am lucky to be surrounded by people who have the same sense of obligation. When you know someone would make great sacrifices for you when called upon, you are more likely to make great sacrifices in return. And that's one way that great teams are built.

File under "Mantra"

People can tell what's important to you by your actions. *Live by your mantra.* Demonstrate your leadership philosophy on a daily basis. Treat every opportunity as if it is your one chance to have some impact and to leave people with an accurate impression of who you are. It may very well be the only shot you ever get. So...what's *your* mantra?

Chapter 11

EMBRACING FAILURE

Own It, and Come Back with a Vengeance

The last place I thought I would find myself in the spring of 2010 was in Nepal. Yet there I was, getting ready to go another round with the big mountain after getting knocked out in 2002. I had really believed that I would never come back. What changed my mind? My girlfriend Meg.

Meg Berté Owen was one of the first people I saw when I got back from Nepal in 2002. She was an amazing friend whom I could share everything with—the good, the bad, and the ugly. Meg could take the bad and the ugly and turn it into something positive, which was part of her magic. She was an optimist by nature. We sat for hours in a coffee shop in New York City, and I told her the whole story—all the details of the trip, about the amazing team of women I had climbed with, and how we'd given it everything we had before coming up short of the summit.

"Well, when are you going to go back and try it again?" she asked.

I responded with absolute clarity, "Uh…I am *not* going to go back and try it again. I pretty much had the whole Everest experience already."

She tilted her head and gave me a look of skepticism. "Come on, I know you better than that. You're going to go back to that mountain."

I rolled my eyes and chuckled "Only if you go with me." Which pretty much put an end to that conversation.

Meg wasn't a mountaineer. But she was one of the most talented athletes I had ever met. She was a brilliant all-American soccer player and captain of her team at Harvard. She was a fierce competitor in every sense of the word. She had to be. When Meg was in her twenties she beat lymphoma—twice. But her lymphoma treatment (chemo, radiation, and stem cell transplant) left her with lung damage, and her compromised lung function meant she could no longer play soccer, the activity she had been most passionate about her whole life.

But Meg didn't let that slow her down. She was always stretching her limits. After a while nothing she did surprised you, because you realized that it was just her nature to live outside of her comfort zone. She found that even with her reduced lung capacity she could ride a bike pretty well, so she put her athletic efforts into cycling. She put so much heart and soul into cycling that in 2005, she was one of two dozen riders chosen to cycle across the country, from San Diego to Washington, DC, with Lance Armstrong (and *no*, she did not use performance-enhancing drugs) as part of the Tour of Hope to raise awareness about cancer research.

And then in 2009, at age thirty-seven, she passed away

duc to complications *from the flu.* She got a lung infection, and because her lungs had been damaged from her lymphoma treatments, she wasn't able to recover. It was one hell of a crusher. Meg was "that girl"—the brilliant, charismatic, funny one who was so high-energy that when you were with her you felt like nothing could stop you. Nothing. She had friends all over the world—literally. After she passed, people started doing things to honor her. They did cycling races and triathlons in places like Japan and Europe. A team ran the New York City Marathon in her honor. I desperately wanted to do something to honor my friend as well, and of course the thing I'm most passionate about is climbing mountains. So I decided to go back to Mount Everest in the spring of 2010, just five and a half months after losing Meg. I engraved her name on my ice axe to make *sure* she was coming with me this time around.

———

April 4, 2010. It was a sunny day in the Khumbu Valley. We were a couple of days into the trek from Lukla to base camp. I was doing my best to just enjoy the hike and not stress out too much about what I would face on Everest's slopes. There is a saying that no one conquers Everest—the mountain merely allows you to climb it. I wondered if I would be allowed to this time.

Part of me envied the people who were just there for the trek. Their trip would be over in two weeks, and they would be back home in their warm beds with running water and good food and *Law & Order: SVU.* The trekkers were all incredibly friendly and enthusiastic. They didn't have to worry about anything too heavy—like surviving a bout with the world's highest peak. I did my best to be cordial to those who tried to make conversation, but my mind was focused on what lay ahead, so sometimes conversations didn't flow all that smoothly.

"First time in Nepal?" a random trekker asked.

I answered with one word: "Nope." I wasn't feeling chatty. I was busy dreading the Khumbu Icefall.

Trekker: "So you've been here before?"

Me: "Yeah."

Trekker: "Here? To the Everest region?"

Me: "Yep."

Trekker: "What were you doing out here?"

Me: "Climbing Everest."

Trekker: "So you've actually climbed this mountain before?"

Me: "Yep, I have."

Trekker: "When?" He wouldn't stop with the questions.

Me: "Two thousand and two."

Trekker: "Wow. So you summited Everest, and you're going to try to do it again?"

Me: "I actually didn't summit on my last trip."

Trekker (stopping in his tracks): "Ohhhh maaaaaaann. Seriously? What a bummer."

Me (still walking): "Yeah, pretty much."

Trekker: "I mean... to spend *all* that time on the mountain... and not get to the top..."

Me: "Well, it happens."

Trekker: "Yeah, but that has really got to eat at you. I mean, that kind of thing has got to haunt you."

Me: "Uh... Only when people like you bring it up." Which was the truth. The guy was relentless!

The truth was, after returning from my 2002 trip, I really

didn't feel like I had any unfinished business on that mountain. Sure, *occasionally* I would get the urge to go back, but usually that happened only when people were giving me a hard time about the trip, which didn't happen often.

But when it did, it would usually go down something like this:

I would be at a dinner party at someone's house, and the host of the party would introduce me by saying, "Oh, hey, I want you to meet my friend Alison—she climbed Mount Everest!"

Then the guy sitting across the table from me would raise his eyebrows and respond, "Oh no way!!!! *All the way to the top?*"

And then, of course, I would have to smile and explain, "Uh, well, no, actually, our team turned around just a couple hundred feet from the top in a storm."

Then he would tilt his head and look at me, as if he felt sorry for me, and say, "Ohhhhhhh...so you *didn't* climb Mount Everest."

Of course I would try to defend myself without actually sounding defensive and without throwing a glass of wine on him. "Well, really, we *did* climb it. My team was awesome—and we got superclose to the top, but ultimately had to turn around in bad weather. The climb was a fantastic experience, etc., etc." I'd explain what happened, how we spent two months on that mountain and just had bad luck with the weather. I'd even go as far as giving him the lecture about how getting to the top is optional and getting down is mandatory.

But he wouldn't buy it. He'd shrug his shoulders and say, "Well, come on...if you weren't at the very top, then you didn't climb it. It doesn't count." His know-it-all tone would annoy me. I could barely refrain from throttling this guy for his arrogance and lack of appreciation for what my team had accomplished.

People who have never climbed a big mountain don't realize that summits are overrated. The cliché about the journey being more important than the destination is right. It's the climb that matters, not the summit. This isn't just sour grapes. I would have loved to have made the summit in 2002, but the fact is, the world doesn't change just because you touched the top of a mountain.

We often look at things through a harsh black-and-white lens—either someone made it to the summit of a mountain or they didn't. They hit their quarterly sales numbers or they didn't. They launched the product on time or they didn't. But before you define success or failure in such concrete terms, you should know that the people who reach the top are often nowhere near the caliber of climber of those who fail to reach the top. This goes for mountains as well as anything else.

Take Chad Kellogg. I met Chad on Everest in 2010. People outside of the climbing community have probably never heard of him. He's incredibly low-key. But he is extraordinary—as a climber and as a person. He has set speed records on mountains all over the world—from Alaska to Kazakhstan. He has also dealt with tragedy along the way. His wife, Lara, died in a climbing accident in Alaska's Ruth Gorge in 2007. Chad was off climbing in a remote area of western China at the time and learned of his wife's death when someone on horseback rode in to his camp and hand-delivered a note to him in his tent.

Just a few months later Chad was diagnosed with colon

cancer. He's suffered many other losses as well, including that of his younger brother, who died of a heart attack.

In 2010, Chad attempted to break the speed record for climbing Everest without supplemental oxygen. Marc Batard of France was the record holder; he made it from base camp to the summit in 22 hours and 29 minutes, then made it back down to base camp in time to set a 36-hour round-trip record. Most climbers who are on their final summit push will spend days going from base camp to the summit, and they'll make use of three or four camps along the route on the way up. Then after they summit, they will spend a night or two at one of the camps on the way back down. Not Chad. His plan was to do it in one push from base camp to the summit and back.

From Chad's blog (www.chadkellogg.com), posted May 26, 2010:

My brain was a bit hypoxic at 26,000 ft. I moved up the fixed lines aware that there were over 150 climbers above me.

The going was slow as I picked my way through the snow-covered rocks. Near the Triangle Face I began to encounter traffic coming down the fixed line. The upward progress was slowed down by all the climbers descending. I soon ran into some of the Argentinian climbers going down. They let me know that the wind and snow increased greatly once I got above the Balcony above the Triangle Face. I continued up slowly and encountered an old climber's body between the rocks. I decided maybe I should take a dexamethasone tablet to reduce the chances of HAPE and HACE. I made it just below the Balcony and decided that Wednesday the 23rd of May was not going to be the day for the speed ascent. I looked at my watch and realized it was 11 a.m. I had been going for nearly nineteen hours. I sat down on a rock at 27,000 ft. and watched as dozens of climbers passed me on their way down to the South Col. The view was obscured by clouds and blowing snow to the North. The morning weather had been good, but the weather had deteriorated as predicted.

I reflected on the combination of problems at hand: wind, snow, traffic, and fatigue. The ascent had a combination of issues that I could only learn from for the next ascent. The focus of the climb had not just been to get to the summit. If that were the case I would have just strapped on a bottle of oxygen and gone to the top. This climb was about meeting the mountain in the most difficult way I could imagine. No porters carrying loads, helping to fix lines, without oxygen from Base Camp to the Summit of the world in a continuous push. I had made it nearly 10,000 vertical feet from Base Camp to the Balcony at 27,000 ft. Although I was disappointed with not achieving the summit, the effort was notable.

"Notable"? He calls this effort *"notable"*? I call it *unbelievable*. Failure to reach the summit—yes. Failure in the grand scheme of life—no. Hell, no! Chad was one of the most skilled and capable climbers on the mountain in 2010.

I caught up with Chad on the hike out at the end of the trip. He shared his training regimen with me—his diet, his workout schedule, his tips for healthy living. I don't think I have ever met anyone who is so disciplined. Had he been climbing with oxygen and supported by Sherpas like 98 percent of the other climbers on the mountain, he would have made it and could probably have gone up and down and tagged the top several times in the same amount of time it would take the rest of us to drag ourselves up there once. But he has no interest in doing things the conventional way.

Chad went back to Everest a second time in 2012, again with the hope of breaking the speed ascent record without oxygen. He was forced to turn back at 28,215 feet/8,600 meters. Once more, just short of the summit. I got an e-mail from him on May 13, 2013, and guess where he was? Back on Everest *again*. Why does he keep going back? In his words: "I have chosen a style of climbing that is so difficult for me that I have had much to learn from the mountain. I believe in the 'old school' technique of the sequential learning curve. You take on the next biggest challenge after you have established the proper base experience."

With each trip to the mountain, Chad was building his knowledge base. And each time he returned, he was better and more prepared. After researching when the weather window looked most promising, Chad set off from base camp at around 3:00 p.m. on May 22, in his third attempt to break the speed record on Mount Everest. By 5:00 a.m. on May 23, he had reached an elevation of over 27,000 feet and was on track to break the record.

From his 2013 blog:

A bit past 5:00 a.m., I realized that the winds on the summit ridge were well into the 40 mph range with spindrift blowing across the Balcony and high into the air off the summit ridge. I knew that, without oxygen, my appendages would not withstand the windchill. Seemingly in unison with my growing apprehension, a radio call came in from our head Sirdar, Phurba. He said that the summit weather was too dangerous for me and he urged us to return to Camp 4. This was the dilemma that I had feared most. I was on pace! Pushing myself for over 14 hours, I was in position to set the speed record on Everest without oxygen. I had seven hours with which to climb the final 1,800 ft. to the summit. I had climbed nearly 10,000 vertical feet above Base Camp to reach an elevation of 27,225 feet.

This was my third attempt at the summit, and I would not get the window. Why was this happening? Everything was going so well up to this point. Deep inside, I knew that the only decision to make was to go back down, but I still wanted to go up. I began to climb again....Another set of climbers began to descend on us, knocking more rocks down on us. It was clear that I could not ignore the signs any longer. With a heavy heart, I made my way slowly back to the South Col....

I have to admit that I'm a bit disappointed that I did not reach the summit on this expedition. The takeaway point from this trip is that the only thing you can hope to control in this life is your mind. I am proud of my effort and the ability to return from this expedition healthy and happy. There will be other climbs and trips to be made because I made the right decisions. I have all my fingers, toes, and appendages. I learned and progressed as an athlete and as a human being. After all, life is about living for each moment. I do not have any regrets, as each moment is a gift.

Finding that sweet spot of perfect weather is always a challenge, especially when you're trying to set a speed record, because you can't sit around in your tent and wait for the winds to die down. Chad has yet to summit Mount Everest. Yet he is one of mountaineering's elite. Few high-altitude climbers can match his strength, speed, and skill. He pushes his limits further and further each time he confronts the mountain. He makes smart decisions about when to push and when to back off, which means he'll have more opportunities to try again in the future. Chad Kellogg is not afraid to fail. With each attempt he comes back stronger. And those are just a few of the many things that make him great.

The lesson here? Don't judge climbers by their summits. I give a hell of a lot more credit to people like Chad, who are willing to push themselves, than to those who always take the easiest path because it's familiar and safe. You'll never improve your skills if you keep following your standard route. And getting out of your comfort zone is not enough; you must take it a step further and learn to be comfortable with discomfort. This is an important part of leader development.

Your chances of failure may increase when you're pushing yourself into unfamiliar territory, but you can't let that deter you. In fact, one of my leadership role models is a polar explorer who is most well-known for his epic—and I do mean *epic*—failure: Ernest Shackleton, who was the leader of the Imperial Trans-Antarctic Expedition, which set out from England in autumn of 1914.

Shackleton had plenty of Antarctic experience prior to setting sail for the world's southernmost continent in August 1914. In 1901 he joined Captain Robert F. Scott on the Discovery Expedition, which was setting off to Antarctica for the purpose of research and exploration. The ship departed London in July 1901 and took five and a half months to reach the Antarctic coast. While the main purpose of the trip was to explore and research the Antarctic environment, Scott, Shackleton, and another man, Edward Wilson, made an effort to trek across Antarctica and set a record for reaching the southernmost point on the continent that anyone had reached—82°17'S.

Shackleton struggled through most of the journey, weakened by poor health and the harsh elements, and Captain Scott ended up sending him home from the expedition while the rest of the men stayed on to continue their work in the region. Shackleton may not have been the strongest member of the Discovery Expedition team, but the experience proved to be invaluable. He then had a much better idea of what the Antarctic environment could throw at him.

Several years later, he set off on the Nimrod expedition, this time as the expedition leader, with the goal of reaching the South Pole. He and his team made it to 88°23'S, which is within 112.2 miles of the South Pole, another new record at the time. As a result of this achievement, he was knighted by King Edward VII. His record would, of course, be broken less than three years later when Norwegian Roald Amundsen and his team reached the geographic South Pole, but Shackleton still had another goal in mind that no one else had yet accomplished—completing a crossing of the Antarctic continent.

Many people are familiar with this part of Shackleton's story—his ship, the *Endurance*, became trapped in pack ice and was eventually crushed, and his team had to survive for more than twenty months in the most extreme conditions known to man. Shackleton and his men were presumed dead. No one believed that human beings could survive in that type of deadly environment. But survive they did. And while the team never even had the opportunity to set foot on the Antarctic continent, Shackleton has been hailed a heroic leader because he managed to get every member of his team back alive. Had he not experienced numerous failures during previous Antarctic expeditions, he might not have been the same type of leader when placed in such seemingly hopeless circumstances.

If Shackleton's leadership abilities were measured solely on whether or not he accomplished his goal of crossing the Antarctic continent, then he would hardly be considered a success. But despite his failure to achieve his goal of crossing the continent, he goes down in history as one of the greatest leaders of all time. The brilliant and heroic skills he demonstrated can never be disputed.

Leaders need to make sure that everyone feels like they have purpose and are contributing to the overall efforts of the team. Shackleton's men never lost hope, in part because he gave every man responsibility for performing particular tasks on a daily basis. As a result, everyone felt like they were a critical part of the expedition. Leaders need to make sure that everyone feels like they have purpose and are contributing to the overall efforts of the team.

Getting people into a routine helps them stay focused in extreme environments when things look bleak. But in order to know who to choose for each task, Shackleton had to know quite a bit about each individual on his team—another important aspect of leadership (as mentioned in chapter 8). He not only had to figure out how to best utilize his strongest and most talented team members, but he also had to prevent the troublemakers from making a grim situation worse by bringing down morale. That meant Shackleton had to assess each man's physical and psychological strengths.

Shackleton never stopped thinking about what would be best for all of his men, even in his absence. Eighteen months into the expedition, when he set out in a twenty-two-foot wooden rowboat to go for help, he had to choose five men to go with him. In making his selections, he wasn't just looking at prospects who would be the strongest rowers; he was also considering who might cause the most trouble if left behind. The six men's open boat voyage across eight hundred nautical miles of the harsh southern Atlantic Ocean was ultimately successful. Shackleton orchestrated a miraculous rescue and, as noted, brought every man on his team home alive.

Looking back at our first attempt on Everest in 2002, when our summit bid was thwarted by bad weather, I remember that we felt a lot of pressure to get to the top. We wanted Ford (our corporate sponsor) to be proud of us and to be glad they had sponsored our trip. Our expedition had a strong media following—more than 450 media outlets covered it. We made the rounds on the *Today* show, CNN, and CNBC, and we were featured on *World News Tonight*, the *CBS Evening News*, and many other programs. We were all over the news before and during the trip, and then CNN did live updates from the mountain throughout the expedition.

We were incredibly grateful for Ford's sponsorship, and we wanted to do everything we could to get them as much positive PR exposure as possible. But that being said, it was often hard to manage all the media demands and also remain focused on the climb. It was an added layer of pressure that gave us even more to worry about.

There would be times when all I wanted to do was sleep, but I had to get up and get everyone out of their tents because some television or radio network wanted a live update or an interview. And then when we came back after the trip, we had to make the rounds on all the television shows that had interviewed us prior to the expedition, and we had to explain about the storm and why we didn't make it to the summit.

Typically, in a situation like ours, you get only one shot at the top, because once you've burned through most of your oxygen supply, you don't have enough left to try it again. Plus, you want to limit the amount of time you spend in the death zone, since your body is basically consuming itself and your brain cells are slowly dying. So you get your shot, you make it or you don't, and then you head home. Disappointing to get that close and then not make it? Sure. But in my book, as long as you come back alive, with all of your fingers and toes, and as friends with your climbing partners—I consider that a damn successful trip.

I worried about what Ford would think about our so-called failure and how it would reflect on them, but then I also thought about how it would reflect on them if something seriously bad had happened to one of us on the trip— the ultimate PR nightmare. In situations where lives are on the line, you always err on the side of safety. And when you are a leader you have to think about how your every move will affect not just you, but also the people around you. It doesn't matter how much blood, sweat, and tears you personally put into something; if the conditions aren't right, you cut your losses, you turn around, and you walk away from the deal. Mount Everest isn't going anywhere. You can always go back. But if you do something *dumb* up there… you may not have the opportunity to go back.

If Ford was disappointed in our performance on the mountain, they certainly didn't show it. Folks from their publicity team met us at LAX with massive bouquets of flowers when we arrived back in the States. After everything we had been through on the mountain, it was so nice to see friendly faces at the airport. Ford even offered me a free Ford Explorer to drive for six months, as a way of thanking me for my efforts as the team captain. It was an incredibly generous gesture. (Unfortunately, I had to turn it down because I could not afford it. Crazy, right? I couldn't afford a *free car*. Sounds ridiculous, I know. The problem was that I would have had to pay for the insurance and also for parking in San Francisco—neither of which were affordable for me at the time. So the "free car" would have cost me about $400–500 a month. God, the irony of that just kills me.)

We must always own our failures. Whether or not those failures were due to factors outside of our control isn't relevant. The important thing is to learn from them. That's what really makes us grow as leaders. When we achieve something that we have worked hard for, too many of us don't take a moment to simply reflect on and analyze things—we just move on to our next challenge or conquest.

But after coming up short and not succeeding in what we set out to accomplish, we're more likely to dissect everything and analyze what went right, what went wrong, and what we should do differently the next time around. Players in team sports watch tapes after each game so they can evaluate those actions that contributed to the win or to the loss. While our own day-to-day performances aren't captured on video (unless we happen to be starring in a television series), we can still take the time at the end of each day or week to review the play-by-play and determine what we need to do to improve.

Often, we're hesitant to even *talk* about failure. Almost as if we're afraid that if we let the word enter our mind, we'll jinx ourselves. One of the many benefits of serving on the Thayer Leader Development Group's board is that I have the opportunity to interact with some of our country's best military and business leaders. We meet twice a year at the Thayer Hotel at West Point and share insights on how we can best cultivate leaders of character in the public and private sectors who can meet the complex challenges of a rapidly evolving business climate. Obviously, there is no single right way to approach leader development, which is what makes the dialogue both interesting and lively.

I am always fascinated by what I learn during these conversations, as few people know more about leading teams in extreme environments than military leaders. Combat is no time for on-the-job training, and there is little room for error.

One of my fellow board members is Brig. Gen. (Ret.) Pete Dawkins, who has accomplished more in his lifetime than just about anyone I have ever met. For starters, he overcame polio as a child. He attended the United States Military Academy, where he was first captain (the top-ranked cadet at West Point) and also captain of the football team, which went undefeated his senior year. By the way, he also played baseball and hockey, although football was where he really focused his abilities. In 1958, he won the Heisman Trophy.

But wait—there's more. Dawkins was awarded a Rhodes scholarship and earned his master's at Oxford (he later picked up another master's and a PhD from Princeton). He pushed himself even harder in his career as an army officer. He completed infantry, parachute, and ranger training. He learned Vietnamese and served in Vietnam. He continued to rise through the military ranks, commanding a company in the famed 82nd Airborne Division, a battalion in Korea, and two brigades—one of which was the 101st Airborne Division (Air Assault), another highly decorated unit. He earned numerous military awards, including two Bronze Stars with Valor (for heroism).

I have met few people in my life who have achieved so much success in so many areas. Pete has been supported through every step of his career by his lovely wife, Judi, to whom he has been married for more than fifty years. They raised two children, daughter Noel and son Sean. Sadly, Sean died at the age of forty-two of a heart defect. They have six grandchildren. This is a guy who has lived, learned, and thrived through situations that most of us could not imagine.

I first met Pete at a TLDG board meeting, shortly after I had appeared on a CNBC program called *Meeting of the Minds: The Future of Leadership*, which centered on how to produce the right kinds of leaders for the twenty-first century. The program was filmed at West Point and my fellow panelists were Jim Owens, CEO of Caterpillar; Anne Mulcahy, CEO of Xerox; Robert Kraft, owner of the New England Patriots; Hank Paulson, former Treasury secretary; Capt. Chesley "Sully" Sullenberger; and Gen. (Ret.) Wesley

Clark. In thinking about where I could add value to this esteemed panel, I figured I would talk about the importance of failure (clearly setting fiscal policy, landing a plane on the Hudson, commanding NATO forces, running a multi-billion-dollar company, and owning a winning Super Bowl franchise weren't on my list of potential topics).

Anyway, I was telling General Dawkins about my experience on the panel and why I thought it was important to discuss failure in the context of leadership. He agreed that failure was indeed an important topic, one that was too often avoided.

The irony was not lost on me that I was talking to one of the most successful human beings to ever grace God's green earth, and we were having a conversation about *failure*. I figured talking to Pete Dawkins about failure was akin to talking to the pope about sex—something he knew existed but happened only to other people. What could this guy possibly know about failure? A lot, surprisingly.

Pete subsequently sent me a copy of an article he had written back when he was a captain. It appeared in the September–October 1965 issue of *Infantry Magazine* and was titled "Freedom to Fail." In the article Pete wrote about the dangers of obsessing over perfection, which creates "a cult of the unerring." He said we tend to hold people who have had perfect track records in high esteem—but often it is those individuals with blemishes on their records who have really pushed themselves and have taken the risks that allow others to succeed. The risk-takers are the ones whose mistakes spur progress. Often, those who have never failed have not pushed themselves enough.

Dawkins wrote, "No man, no matter how talented or

inspired, is perfect. If he is to pursue a bold and vigorous path rather than one of conformity and acquiescence, he will sometimes err. Greatness can ultimately succeed only if such men are granted the freedom to fail." If we take risks without the fear of being judged when we fail, then we set ourselves up for success when it really counts.

In general, we are not a failure-tolerant society, which is ironic, considering our country's entrepreneurial and innovative roots. But a lack of failure tolerance can stifle progress and creativity. Very often, we hesitate to take risks because we fear potential failure. Trust me, if Pete Dawkins is okay with failure, we should be, too. Whether the risk we take is climbing a mountain or accepting a position that will stretch our intellect, demand new skills, and require hard work, it is always easier to avoid the risks—unless we have failed before. There is something about surviving past setbacks that increases our willingness to risk again.

———

May 23–24, 2010

11:00 p.m. We have lost radio contact with base camp.

They have no idea what the weather conditions are up here in the death zone at 26,000 feet, so in order to not worry our friends and loved ones back home who are reading the cybercast online, the base camp staff reports that the weather is pretty good but that there is an "increased chance of precipitation." The reality is that just about every base camp manager of every major expedition on the mountain is worried about us, and many stay awake the entire night in their attempts to check in on us. It's a tight group on the mountain. Everyone pulls together to help everyone. *The good folks do, anyway....*

We leave camp at the South Col and start climbing in the howling winds that have been battering our tents for the past few hours. The snow is really coming down now. It's pitch-dark, but you need to protect your eyes so that your eyeballs don't freeze, so I'm wearing clear goggles because if my corneas freeze I am done. I know of several people who have had to turn around close to the top because of frozen eyeballs. Within minutes my goggles fog up and are worthless. *Arghhh.* I scrap the goggles and just try to close my eyes for a few extra milliseconds in between steps. I am getting pelted in the face with snow. Hard. *Not really appreciating the free microdermabrasion.* I can feel little icicles forming on my eyelashes. *There is no way we are going to climb for long in this weather.*

We keep moving. Lakpa Rita Sherpa is first in line, followed by Chhewang. If Chhewang makes it all the way to the top he will be one summit short of tying the record for the most Everest summits.* After Chhewang there is me, followed by a few others who have also chosen to continue despite the perilous conditions. Lakpa and Chhewang are breaking trail and have to kick in steps, since there is a decent amount of new snow covering the trail. Their steps are too big for me. My legs cannot reach that far. Trying to use their steps is exhausting, so I do my best to kick in my own, which is also exhausting. *I hate being short.*

---

* Tragically, Chhewang Nima Sherpa died five months later in Nepal while climbing Baruntse.

Very few climbers are going for the summit tonight, because the weather is not ideal.

The upside is that we won't have to deal with crowds on the fixed lines or at the Hillary Step. We have now been climbing for about two hours. I look up and see a big group of headlamps ahead of us. This is a good sign and gives me hope, because it means that there are other people up here who feel like this mountain is climbable in these conditions. It takes me a minute to realize that the headlamps are not pointing uphill but are pointing toward us. *That's not the way to the summit, you guys.* My hope starts to disintegrate. The headlamps finally catch us as they make their way down. It's a large group—maybe about twenty people who had left camp about two hours before I left my tent, and their guide tells us that the weather conditions are too extreme for them to continue, so they are calling it quits and heading back down to Camp 4 at the South Col. His last words to us: "I hope we don't regret this decision." The group doesn't look human. They look like zombies. But then again, no one really looks human up here.

His words reverberate in my head, bouncing back and forth from ear to ear. I know those words and that feeling oh so well from 2002, when our team turned back just a few hundred feet from the summit. Up here, you always have to err on the side of safety, because getting to the top is optional. Getting down is mandatory. Still, I remembered the feeling of disappointment of not making it to the top like it was yesterday, even though it was eight years ago. But disappointment is a natural part of life. Dying in the mountains is not. I had to stop thinking about the group descending and focus on performing the best I could during the next eight to ten hours of climbing.

Part of me now hopes we also will turn around in the crappy weather, because the ferocious winds and snow are making me nervous. *I don't know if I can do this. I want to be able to blame the weather rather than my own weakness if I do not make it.* But we keep climbing. I'm still unsure of whether I'm happy or sad about that. Every part of me is numb. Including my feelings.

Visibility is horrible. I know my pal Meg would tell me to ignore the pain and discomfort and to just put my head down and keep taking steps uphill. She was a fighter. *Much more so than I am.* Having her name engraved on my ice axe gives me superpowers. *Meg, I miss you. I didn't even get to say good-bye....*

We stop at the Balcony—27,500 feet—to switch out our oxygen bottles. If your equipment malfunctions, your hopes of getting to the top will be dashed. So many things can go wrong. *I don't need another oxygen tank problem like the one I experienced last time.* We have been climbing for about five hours. I am glad it's dark because I think I would be even more intimidated if I could see the steepness of the route. We keep climbing throughout the night and into the early morning. The weather seems to be in a steady state of sh*tty. Then we reach a 90-foot vertical rock pitch. *What the??? No one told me about this!!! Son of a...* Apparently the fixed lines usually go around this section of the route, but this year the lines go straight up and over the intimidating, towering rock wall. One by one, so do we. I am out of breath, even with my oxygen tank feeding me. One step at a time, we are getting closer to where we want to be. I think about the fact that we are climbing at an elevation where airplanes fly.

We reach the South Summit—28,700 feet. This was where I turned around back in 2002. It was the highest point I had reached on this mountain. *I don't remember ever being here at all. I have no idea how I even got this far on my last trip. I have no idea how I got this far on this trip.* I am feeling totally dehydrated and I need calories. It's so cold and the terrain has been steep, so we haven't stopped much for food or water.

Suddenly, someone is right next to me. Michael Horst, mountain guide extraordinaire, unclipped himself from the rope to climb up alongside me. Michael was supposed to be climbing with a woman who had hired him to be her private guide, but she had to pull out of the trip early and isn't getting her shot at the summit. Her loss is most certainly our gain, because now he is climbing with our group. He pulls off his mask and starts to talk to someone. *Wait—he is talking to me. What could possibly be this important?* "Hey, Alison...I need you to promise me something." He has to yell so I can hear him over the wind. *What the hell do you want, Michael? This is no time to be asking me for anything. Don't you get that it is all I can do to put one foot in front of the other right now? I am not strong and tough like you are. I wish I had your long legs and your powerful lungs.* I am huffing and puffing. I reply, "What?" He is still without his oxygen mask as he climbs closer to me and speaks: "I need you to promise me...that you are going to go farther than *this.*"

Michael is referring to the spot on the mountain where we are standing, the South Summit, my previous high point. I start to laugh but am choking back tears at the same time. I don't know why I am so emotional. I guess knowing that someone else up on that mountain actually cared about my success was an overwhelming feeling. The mountain can be very isolating. Even when there are people climbing right next to you. Michael and I shake hands on the promise. I never break a promise to a friend. *Now I have to keep climbing....*

The route feels deserted. Is this good? *Yes. No crowds, no bottlenecks.* Or is this bad? *Maybe we are fools to think we can keep going in this weather.* I see a climber and a Sherpa in front of us. The climber is barely moving. I get closer and recognize her red down suit. It is Lei Wang, a woman I met on my way to Camp 3. We had chatted on the steep Lhotse Face. I am excited to see that she is on her way to the summit as well. "Lei, Lei? Are you okay?" She doesn't answer. Or maybe she did—but I couldn't hear her over the wind. Up in the death zone, it's very easy for your mind to go to the darkest place. A wave of fear rushes over me. But then Lei starts to move very slowly. *Phew! She is fine! Probably just taking it slow.* We carefully pass her, but I keep a mental picture of where she is on the route. I am still worried. I turn back one last time...she is moving again. Okay then, onward....

We keep climbing. I look down. Everest's Southwest Face on one side and Kangshung Face on the other. One drop is 8,000 feet and the other is 10,000. *Slipping is not an option.*

Up ahead, the Hillary Step. Forty feet of damn-close-to-vertical rock and perhaps the most dreaded part of a summit bid. *But the crappy weather, poor visibility, freezing temperatures, hypoxia, chances of frostbite, altitude sickness, and falling thousands of feet to your death are all right up there, too.*

I get over the Hillary Step. I keep moving. One... step...at...a...time. I see something up ahead. A mound of snow, prayer flags, a small statue. I think I am hallucinating....

8:10 a.m. I am standing on the summit of Mount Everest. *Could I really be here? I am waiting for Ashton Kutcher to jump out and tell me I have been punk'd.* People start hugging me and congratulating me because I have just completed climbing the Seven Summits (highest peak on each continent) and skiing to both Poles, an accomplishment known as the Adventure Grand Slam. *If nothing else, this should be good for a free breakfast at Denny's.*

It still hasn't really hit me that I am where I am. I look around and try to take in the view, but there is no view because the clouds have completely closed in. *Now it hits me. I am here.* I am standing on the very spot where legends have stood before—the adventurers I have been reading about for years, the ones I have admired and idolized, true trailblazers in their day. I wondered what they must have been feeling when they reached this point—29,029 feet/8,848 meters.

———

So, on May 24, 2010, I made it to the summit of Mount Everest in honor of my girlfriend Meg. After turning back at the South Summit—just a few hundred feet from the top in 2002—I swore I would never try again. Part of me can't believe I actually did try again. And trust me, there were many moments of self-doubt. But somehow I found myself on the top of that mountain.

I am often asked what it was like—to go back to that mountain eight years later, after everything I had been through, and finally stand on top of the highest mountain in the world. I can honestly tell you (wait for it...deep breath...) *it just wasn't that big a deal.* Heavy sigh. Think about it for a moment. It's *just a mountain.* It's nothing more than a big ol' pile of rock and ice. And you are only on the summit for a very short time. You spend two months climbing that mountain, and only a few minutes at the very top. I was up there for thirty minutes. Standing on top of a mountain is not important, and the people who stand on top of Mount Everest are no better than the people who turn around short of the summit. Because climbing mountains isn't about standing on the top of a pile of rock and ice for a few minutes—it's about the *lessons you learn along the way* and how you are going to use that knowledge and experience to *better* yourself going forward.

I promise you that plenty of better, stronger, more skilled, much more deserving climbers than Alison Levine didn't make it that day—for whatever reason. Most of them turned back because of the weather. But because I had that failed experience from 2002 under my belt, I knew what it felt like to get beat up and knocked around on that mountain. I knew what it was like to get the snot kicked out of me high up on the summit ridge in a storm. And I wasn't afraid of that this time around. I knew what my risk tolerance was, and I knew what my pain threshold was. Had I not had that failed experience eight years prior, I very well might have turned around when most others did.

Shortly after my return, the *New York Times* ran an article about my completion of the Adventure Grand Slam on the front page of the sports section. They published a photo of me at the summit, which resulted in phone calls from dozens of friends congratulating me on the accomplishment. "Hey, I'm looking at a great photo of you in the *Times*!" they would say. But there was a lot more to that photo than what they could see. That photo was actually very *misleading*. Because while people did see me standing at the top of Mount Everest, let me tell you what they *didn't* see: the sponsors who helped to fund my trip, the logistics providers who got all the permits in order, the amazing team of Sherpas who helped ferry loads up and down the mountain, the incredible guides who gave me direction along the way, the friends who helped me train before I left for Nepal, the loved ones who gave me their moral support leading up to the trip...I could go on and on. There were a lot of people who played a part in my reaching that summit; you just can't see them in the photo. Always remember: nobody gets to the top of Mount Everest by themselves. Nobody.

File under "Failure Tolerance"

Considering that extreme environments are exceedingly demanding and require us to push ourselves well beyond our everyday comfort zones, we must give ourselves permission to fail—even as we do all the required mental and physical preparation to succeed. Failure in and of itself is not a bad thing. But failing to learn from it is inexcusable. You take what you learn on one peak and carry it with you to the next peak so you know what you need to tweak or do differently on the next climb. And the beauty of knowledge and experience is that it doesn't weigh anything—it actually makes your load lighter.

AFTERWORD

My fascination with the art of leadership began before I ever strapped on my first pair of crampons. I've been interested in the topic ever since I held my first position in government.

After a hard-fought electoral win, I was voted into office at a younger age than most politicians. The campaign trail had been rough on my family and me. I had to gather enough signatures to get my name on the ballot, and then I relied on good old grassroots campaigning in order to defeat my opponent. I didn't have much of a budget. My family helped me make posters for walls and lawns, and buttons for people to wear on their shirts. I tried to meet with as many of my constituents as I could in the hope of convincing them that I deserved their support on election day.

I learned the art of shaking hands and looking people in the eye and asking for exactly what I wanted: their votes. And I got them. And at the ripe old age of thirteen, I became the student body president of my elementary school.

The voters to whom I was accountable were the kids enrolled at Madison Meadows, a public school in the sweatbox known as Phoenix, Arizona—my hometown. I distinctly remember the swearing-in ceremony and how I felt, because the thought racing through my mind was: *What the hell am I supposed to do now?* Sure, I had been vice president of the school the previous year, when I was a seventh grader. My campaign slogan back then was "Place Your Money, Roll the Dice, Vote Alison Levine for Vice." I figured the *President* after *Vice* would be inferred (although those who knew me as a kid probably had a different interpretation). But most vice presidents don't really do anything, so my role as veep didn't necessarily prepare me for anything that might come my way as president.

I don't think I left behind a lot of concrete achievements as elementary school president, to tell the truth (sorry about that, guys!). But I did feel a responsibility to look out for the kids on the playground. When something bad happened—someone pushed someone else off the monkey bars, or a kid jumped off one end of the teeter-totter and sent the other kid flying off his or her seat—I felt compelled to intervene.

But here's the thing: looking back, I realize that I should have felt compelled to intervene even if I weren't the president. It's important to keep reminding ourselves that it's our responsibility to look out for one another. It's never too early to get into that mind-set. We should start teaching our kids about leadership in elementary school.

Every mission we undertake in our lives should not only be about reaching the goal, but also about the people we affect and the lessons we learn along the way. The *journey* is where we find perspective. My hope is that the insights I've shared from my various expeditions will inspire and enable people to embrace and master a leadership mind-set, which is as much about *how* we reach our goals as it is about actually reaching them.

Thank you for reading this book, for joining me on my

adventures, and for allowing me to share my thoughts on leadership with you. Maybe you've worked for decades to become a good leader. Or maybe your work is just starting. Either way, the lessons you learn and practice will affect all aspects of your life. I believe that if you make yourself a better leader, you will make the world a better place for yourself and your teammates—the other inhabitants of our beautiful, challenging planet.

Never let failure discourage you. Every time you get to the base of a mountain (literal or metaphorical), you're presented with a new opportunity to challenge yourself, to push your limits beyond what you thought possible, to learn from climbers on the trail ahead of you, and to take in some amazing views. Your performance on the mountain you climbed last week or last month or last year doesn't matter—because it's all about what you are doing *right now*.

I know that I did my *absolute best* to get to the summit of Mount Everest on May 24, 2010. I also know that there will always be more mountains to climb…so going forward, after each one, I have to be even *better.*

INDEX

acclimatization, 25, 46, 50, 87. *See also* altitude sickness
  climbing away from the summit and, 19, 25–30, 48
  climbing schedule and, 123, 131
  defined, 28
  improper, altitude sickness and, 29–30
  physical changes and, 29
  routes to the summit and, 19–20
Aconcagua, Mount, 129
Adventure Grand Slam, xxii, 224, 226
agility, 31, 82–84
air travel
  helicopter evacuation, Afghanistan, 163, 166, 167–68
  helicopter transport, to and from Everest, xv, 48, 49, 50–51, 66
  high-altitude landings/takeoffs dangers, 20, 48, 51
  Himalayan risks, 20, 51
  Lukla Airport as most dangerous, 20
  Nepal plane crashes, 51
Ali, Muhammad, 119
Alpine Ascents International expedition (2010), xv–xx
  April 18 journal entry, 84–87
  May 10 journal entry, 46–49
  May 17 journal entry, xv–xvi
  May 21 journal entry, xvi–xvii
  May 22 journal entry, xvii
  May 23 journal entry, xvii–xx
  May 23–24 journal entry, 218–25
  author joins, 199, 201
  author reaches the summit, 224–25
  climbers with, 47–49, 85–86
  company's reputation, 44
  decision to attempt the summit, xix–xx
  dissimilarity of climbers, 48–49
  Horst and, 14, 222–23
  Sherpas, xviii, xix, 47, 50–51, 219
  staff and guides, 47, 50–51, 86, 222

team dynamics of, 44–52
team ego missing from group, 52
weather, xv, xvi, xviii, xix, xx, xxi, 46–47, 218, 219, 220, 221
Altitude Junkies, xviii
altitude sickness, 28, 29–30
  Acute Mountain Sickness (AMS), 29–30
  avoiding, 30
  dexamethasone for, xviii
  High Altitude Cerebral Edema (HACE), xviii, 30, 206
  High Altitude Pulmonary Edema (HAPE), 30, 206
American Alpine Club, David A. Sowles Memorial Award, 44
American Women's Everest Expedition (2002), 21–22, 191
  author as team captain, xx, 7, 71, 212–14
  author's preparation for, 3–4, 6–9
  in Breckenridge, CO, 37–38
  corporate sponsor sought, 6, 71–73
  decision to turn back, xx–xxi, 213–14
  failure to reach summit, 44, 199, 202–4, 212–14, 220, 222
  Ford as sponsor, xx, 34, 43, 213
  Legate's death and, xvi, 23
  media following of, 212–13
  media tour, 37
  performance ego and, 42–43
  relationships and networking and, 69–75
  team building, 38–39
  team ego, xii, 43–44, 45, 49, 52
  team members, 36
  team recruitment, 33–36
Amundsen, Roald, 15–16, 210
Angell, Jared, 166, 172
Antarctica, 101–19. *See also* South Pole
  Amundsen-Scott South Pole Station, 118
  Discovery Expedition, 210

233

ABOUT THE AUTHOR

Alison Levine is a history-making polar explorer and mountaineer who has survived subzero temperatures, hurricane-force winds, sudden avalanches...and a career on Wall Street. In addition to having served as the team captain of the first American Women's Everest Expedition, she has climbed the Seven Summits (highest peak on each continent) and skied to both the North and South Poles—an achievement known as the Adventure Grand Slam. Her success in extreme environments is noteworthy given she has undergone three heart surgeries and suffers from Raynaud's disease, which causes the arteries that feed her fingers and toes to collapse in cold weather—leaving her at extreme risk for frostbite.

Levine served three years as an adjunct professor at the United States Military Academy at West Point in the Department of Behavioral Sciences and Leadership. A sought-after consultant and keynote speaker on the subject of leadership development, she has addressed audiences ranging from Fortune 500 companies to the World Economic Forum in Davos. She was featured on the CNBC program *Meeting of the Minds: The Future of Leadership*, alongside other notable leaders such as Gen. (Ret.) Wesley Clark, former NATO Supreme Allied Commander; Henry Paulson, former Treasury secretary; and Robert Kraft, CEO and chairman of the New England Patriots.

In addition to having tackled some of the most challenging environments in the outdoors, Levine has also spent more than two decades in the business world. Her professional career has encompassed health care, technology, and finance. She serves on the boards of the Fuqua/Coach K Center on Leadership and Ethics at Duke University and the Thayer Leader Development Group at West Point. She was a contributing author to the book *Leadership in Dangerous Situations: A Handbook for the Armed Forces, Emergency Services, and First Responders* (Naval Institute Press).

A native Arizonan, Levine holds a BA from the University of Arizona and an MBA from Duke University. When she is not on a remote mountain peak or on the road lecturing, she spends her time in her hometown of Phoenix and in San Francisco with her partner, Pat, and their dog, Trooper.

**BUSINESS
PLUS**

Recognized as one of the world's most prestigious business imprints, Business Plus specializes in publishing books that are on the cutting edge. Like you, to be successful we always strive to be ahead of the curve.

Business Plus titles encompass a wide range of books and interests—including important business management works, state-of-the-art personal financial advice, noteworthy narrative accounts, the latest in sales and marketing advice, individualized career guidance, and autobiographies of the key business leaders of our time.

Our philosophy is that business is truly global in every way, and that today's business reader is looking for books that are both entertaining and educational. To find out more about what we're publishing, please check out the Business Plus blog at:

www.businessplusbooks.com